INTERNATIONAL

Showgirl

GAYNOR SCOTT

A Memoir

INTERNATIONAL SHOWGIRL

For My Beautiful Children, Dan and Genie

This book is an accurate account of how I personally experienced these events and remember them during my career as a showgirl dancer. If anyone recalls these events differently, then this is because we experience things differently. A few names have been changed for the purpose of privacy. I believe that I have represented everyone honestly and fairly.

Table of Contents

CHAPTER ONE

Staffordshire, England

One of my earliest childhood memories was my first visit to what was to become my dancing school, The Tweedale Academy of Dancing. I was four years old. Little did any of us know then how this would shape my life.

The Tweedale sisters, Miss Susan and Miss Veronica, ran the Tweedale Dance Academy.

The dancing school was in an old building in the center of Longton in Stoke-on-Trent.

Longton was around a 15-minute drive from Forsbrook, the pretty little village where we lived. We went up a flight of wooden stairs, through an old painted door, and on the first floor there were two changing rooms and two dance studios, a toilet, a small stock area where you could buy ballet shoes, jazz shoes, leotards and tights, and the lobby area where Mrs. Tweedale sat; she was the elderly mother of the two teaching sisters. Mrs. Tweedale used to hold court in the small lobby area and enjoy gossiping with the parents whilst selling drinks and snacks and taking fees for lessons from the parents.

Every Saturday, I would go to my ballet class, gradually working my way up through the I.D.T.A. grade exams.

Miss Veronica was a strict teacher; most of us were a bit scared of her and she was extremely serious in ballet classes, but she was an excellent teacher. When exam time came around, I always achieved very well in my dance exams, gaining the top awards—Highly Commended or Honours—which I was somehow always surprised about, since Miss Veronica never made me feel that I was going to do well!

For ballet, we wore pale pink tunics and matching headbands to keep our hair tidy, as well as white ballet tights with soft, pink, leather ballet shoes. After a few years, once we were older and proficient enough, we were allowed to start Pointe work.

Pointe work was *the* most exciting thing in ballet. We were measured for our pink satin pointe shoes and they had to be ordered especially for each of us individually. I was so desperate and excited for them to arrive. I could not wait and would lie awake at night dreaming about dancing in my pointe shoes.

Our poor feet were not so excited though; there was much bleeding once we started doing pointe work. Dancers' feet are far from pretty beneath our satin ballet shoes. We had to bathe our feet in surgical spirit every night to harden the skin on our toes. It was all worth it though; the feeling of dancing in satin ballet shoes on pointe was just magical and when we saw our own feet in the dance studio mirrors, it elevated and inspired us to dance to another level.

On Mondays I started to attend more dance classes which I loved: Modern Jazz and a Tap dance class. The added bonus was that to attend these dance classes on a Monday, I was actually allowed to leave my school, Blythe Bridge High School, 30 minutes early to be able to catch the train from Blythe Bridge and take the 6-minute journey to the next station, Longton. I always felt so happy skipping out of school early to go and dance.

It was obviously expensive for my parents to pay for all these dance classes and dance clothing required, so I'm forever grateful that they gave me that opportunity. Dad was originally from Jersey, in the Channel Islands. Our family can be traced back to the 13th Century within the small Island.

He and Mum met while Mum was in Jersey on holiday with her family. Dad was aged 15 and Mum was 14. They kept in touch by writing letters. Dad came to study at London University and graduated as a Civil Engineer. Mum was from Surrey, and she graduated from Wimbledon Technical College and worked in various offices in London. She had several interesting office jobs, at a recording studio and a TV station to mention a few; she has always been a creative person at heart, extremely gifted at playing the piano. Like many women at that time though, once she married, she then worked full time as a housewife and mother bringing up myself, my older brother Adrian, who we call Adey, and our younger brother David, who we call Chalky.

First Professional Show, Age 6

Dancing and shows became my whole life and passion. I was always auditioning and rehearsing for a local show outside of school. At age 6, I landed my first paid role in a Professional Christmas Pantomime, *Mother Goose,* at the Gaumont Theatre in Hanley, Stoke-on-Trent.

Mum had seen the auditions advertised in the local daily Sentinel newspaper, looking for children to appear alongside well-known TV stars of the time. The week before the audition Mum encouraged me to practice my audition song by getting me to stand at the top of the stairs in the hall and sing out loudly so that they could hear me down in the lounge. Dad wasn't too enthusiastic about any of it, knowing that there would be thousands of children from all over the city applying for around 10 places in the show, but since I wanted to try, he dropped Mum and me at the theatre with our packed lunch for the day on a Saturday morning and we signed in and waited our turn. He was probably happy to have the house to himself anyway so that he could watch sport on TV quietly.

We waited for hours and hours sat in the auditorium of the theatre, watching the other auditionees on stage until it was finally my turn to go up on the stage with a group of other hopefuls. We stood in a line at the front of the stage and I sang in my loudest voice into the microphone when it was my turn and smiled out into the audience. I was called back the following day for further and final auditions and, after many more hours, told the exciting news that I had been chosen!

I remember going to bed so excited to be in the show and what's more, we were to be paid £4 per week, which was a lot of money for a six-year-old.

Miss Veronica and Miss Susan were of course delighted when they heard that I had been chosen to appear in the professional pantomime. It reflected well on them when any of their pupils were successful and of course old Mrs. Tweedale enjoyed boasting about my success in the refreshment area I heard.

There was great anticipation across the city for the opening of *Mother Goose* and lots of photos in the local newspaper of us with the stars of the show and adverts for tickets.

Many of the teachers and my friends at school excitedly told me that they had seen me in the newspaper. The pantomime opened to great reviews and packed audiences. I couldn't wait to get to the theatre to perform and loved looking out at the jam-packed auditorium at the sea of happy faces.

Following on from the *Mother Goose* pantomime, I now had the bug to be in shows and on stage at every possible opportunity. I wanted to audition for anything available.

My next show that I was chosen for was *The King and I,* which was put on by the North Staffordshire Amateur Operatic Society. They were well known to be the best local Amateur Company and their shows were always a very high standard. The well-known pop star Robbie Williams is also from Stoke-on-Trent and started out performing with them, although sadly our paths never crossed in the same shows.

I was successful in my audition again and this time appeared as one of the King's children in *The King and I* at the Queens Theatre in Burslem. Burslem was the other side of the city from where we lived around 40 minutes in a car and since Mum did not drive, we spent hours travelling across the city to and from rehearsals on buses, having to wait around and change buses 2 or 3 times, often reaching home quite late at night. Mum was always so supportive and encouraging though, since she knew that I loved being in the shows. I would fall into bed before getting up for school the next morning.

Following that, I auditioned successfully and appeared in their next production, which was *Fiddler on The Roof*. I was cast as Tevyes' youngest daughter, Bielke. This was probably my favourite amateur dramatic show ever. I loved all of the songs and the very dramatic and emotional story and best of all, having to wear a long, straight wig, so glamorous and different from my short, curly hair that I always hated and tried to straighten.

Not long after *Fiddler* finished, we were phoned by Miss Veronica telling us that the dancing school had been chosen to provide children for a professional pantomime production of *Babes in the Woods* at Jollees in Longton, Stoke-on-Trent.

Jollees was the largest capacity cabaret venue in the whole of the UK at that time; it was very plush inside and hosted headlining acts. Outside, it was anything but plush, located over a large bus and coach station, apparently some of the top acts were initially reluctant to appear there, but once their peers started to perform they all came. Visitors included members of the Royal family. It also hosted events such as the World Professional Darts championship.

Babes in the Woods was being produced and directed by a show business legend from London called Kenny Earle. It was the end of our family summer holiday in UK; we were by the seaside somewhere and Mum had been asked to call Miss Veronica on a certain date about the forthcoming pantomime. Mum was on the phone and I was straining to hear. Mum came off the phone excited and told me that they had chosen me to be one of the two lead babes; there was to be a boy babe called Peter and a girl babe called Polly and I had been chosen to be Polly. Miss Veronica was frantically saying to Mum, "Under no circumstances cut Gaynor's hair; they want it long and curly." For once, maybe due to the extra length weighing down the curls so that they were long and pretty ringlets, I actually did really like my long curly hair.

The celebrities at the time who were appearing were Ivy Tilsley from *Coronation Street* and a few others who I don't really recall. Ivy was a really sweet lady and we became very close; at the end of the run on the last night she gave me a beautiful silver charm, which I have to this day on my silver charm bracelet. I remember that she always seemed to be very jolly, drinking and smoking a lot backstage, but most of the entertainers did.

My favourite thing backstage at Jollees were the white walls in the backstage area where visiting performing celebrities had autographed and signed their names. We were allowed to sign our names too since we were appearing and performing there, how exciting I thought seeing *my* name alongside people who were actual celebrities at the time.

The following year, Mum heard on the radio that they were going to put on a professional production of *The Sound of Music* in the West End of London at the Apollo Victoria Theatre. Mum asked me if I wanted to go and audition to which I replied yes obviously.

We set off super early in the morning from Stoke-on-Trent railway station, dressed in my best cute dress and shoes and armed with snacks; we guessed that it would be a long day. When we arrived in London we got off the train and walked to the theatre and then we saw the biggest queue that I've ever seen in my life. I don't know how many hours we actually waited outside on the pavement in the long, snaking queue, but eventually it was my turn to go in through the Stage door and audition.

Parents were not allowed in for the actual audition part and had to wait outside. I was ushered onto the stage and we all stood in a long line across the stage. In front of us in the auditorium sat a panel of judges from the production. As we started to sing "Doh a Deer," there was a lady that walked behind us with a clipboard. At the end we were thanked and dismissed other than any lucky children who were tapped on the head with the clipboard who then were called back for a second audition.

After hours of queuing, the actual audition on stage took around 3 minutes and was all over. They quickly ushered us off the other side of the stage and ushered the next group on.

Some of the other children were crying and I remember feeling deeply disappointed myself too. It was a memorable experience and I'm so grateful that my Mum always encouraged me and gave me all of these wonderful opportunities to try to follow my dream. I'm sure that she really enjoyed being part of all the excitement too, I have fond memories from that special and exciting day and recently went to the Apollo Victoria theatre to see *Wicked* with my husband Tom and son Danny, It was so funny thinking that I had been on that very stage as a young girl auditioning.

At school, I was being given a lead role in the school Christmas play each year. I suppose the teachers knew that I was a safe bet at learning my lines and not being too nervous on the night. Some of the other parents might have been fed up seeing Gaynor Smith up front each time though!

I loved my school, The Beeches Junior School in Forsbrook village. It was a traditional Church of England school, we grew up with daily assemblies, singing hymns and saying prayers and learning the national anthem. My own children don't recognize any hymns if we are ever in a church, since schools no longer seem to teach this now. Interestingly, my daughter Genie is currently at school in Dubai and they sing the UAE national anthem at school every week, which I think is valuable.

Each year at The Beeches Junior school, the children were given the chance to vote and choose their school Captains from the final year. There was a boy and girl Captain and a boy and girl Vice Captain. I had the honour of being chosen as the Vice Captain. Part of our role as Captains was to write and conduct our school assemblies once a week, which I loved. Together with the boys and Maxine the Captain, my good friend, we would write our own assemblies, prayers and choose the hymns to sing. Then we would stand on the stage at the front of the school hall and lead the school assembly, which I loved, it was another chance to perform in a way, a different type of production.

One Christmas, I remember spending the holidays with my cousin Penny who was staying with us, making up our own show in my bedroom. I loved choosing the perfect costumes for us to wear. We rehearsed for a few days and then had the ingenious idea that we would instruct Mum, Dad and my big brother Adey to come and watch us and we made them pay for the privilege! We charged them a few pence each for a ticket in my bedroom. They all sat on the bed and we fed them Christmas Quality Streets chocolates at the interval.

Having had so much fun doing this, Mum suggested that we offer to do our show at an old people's care home nearby. Mum phoned them and asked if they would like us to come and do our little show for some of the residents in the nearby village of Cheadle. They accepted our offer and we performed for the elderly patients and staff, but this time didn't charge them or feed them Quality Streets.

At home I was obsessed with watching *The Kids From Fame* TV show about a performing arts school in New York, dancing around the lounge turning it into my imaginary dance studio singing the theme tune and reciting the mantra *"You want fame, well, fame costs and right here is where you start paying, in sweat!"* I was also taking piano lessons, which I enjoyed, but I was never as naturally gifted as my mum. At school I was busy extending my performing skills too, by learning to play the flute and then the bassoon for a while and I studied Guildhall Drama and took drama exams. Everything I did was linked to performing.

The Gaumont theatre had closed, so the Theatre Royal in Hanley was now hosting most professional and amateur shows in Stoke-on-Trent and I performed in a few shows there. One was *Goldilocks and the Three Bears* and we had real Russian bears in the show. This would never be allowed these days thankfully. At the time as a child, I didn't really think about how cruel it was for these poor, beautiful bears being kept backstage in tiny cages.

During my last Christmas at school, aged 16, I was chosen by Miss Veronica to be one of the dancers in *Aladdin* a professional Christmas pantomime at this theatre. I immediately befriended the older girls who were all paid professional dancers and asked them every question I could possibly think of.

Lesley and Sally and their lives seemed so exciting and glamorous to me as they talked about their various dancing contracts, one having just returned from Japan and another having just returned from dancing around the world on cruise ships. This was exactly what I wanted to do, dance and travel the world and be paid for it. They told me that they bought *The Stage* newspaper every week—this is a British weekly newspaper (and now website) for the entertainment industry and has all the latest auditions for big west end shows, cabarets, pantomimes, theatre work, cruise ships and dancing jobs all around the world and this was how they all found most of their dancing contracts. Other than that, they registered with a few agents who could also find jobs and would take a commission, usually from the venue or employer.

I immediately asked Mum if we could please order The Stage at the local newsagents in our village, which she did. I could not wait each week when The Stage newspaper dropped through our letter box, excitedly looking through all of the auditions in exotic and exciting places like, Paris, Madrid, Egypt, Tokyo, South Korea, along with UK summer seasons and pantomimes. I would daydream about being able to apply for these dancing jobs all around the world as soon as I left school.

Fashion Shows and Beauty Queens

Some of my friends from dancing school were a few years older than me and they were starting to compete in local beauty contests and do some modeling in local fashion shows too. Helen was one of these dancing friends and she encouraged me to get involved too as soon as I turned 16. I was excited to be included and learning.

I started modeling in the local fashion shows with Helen and doing promotion work too, from wedding dress fashion shows, to launching new Mercedes cars at car garages, launching the new Beaujolais wine and promoting local Radio stations at their road shows, we had lots of fun and earning money was a such a huge bonus for me since I was still in my final year at school, preparing for my exams.

It probably did not help my studying much, looking back. My school teachers and careers officers were all unenthusiastic when I told them that I wanted to be a professional dancer and tried to get me to think about doing other options. I certainly had the academic ability. I achieved well at school and no doubt without the distractions of dancing shows and fashion shows If I had applied more of my time to studying, I could have achieved even more academically, but all I wanted to do was be a performer, that was my dream and goal.

One problem I really noticed when I started modeling in these fashion shows was that my ears stuck out too much. I had always had lots of thick hair, which helped disguise this most of the time, but when we had to wear headdresses or have our hair up, I could only see one thing: my sticking-out ears. Eventually, my parents allowed me to have otoplasty surgery to pin my ears back, since they could see that it was perhaps going to hinder me getting work in such an image conscious industry.

This was a very big gesture from my father who was never one to part with his money easily; he was very frugal most of the time, always seeking out the lowest prices and best deals everywhere for everything, he always said that it was because they had nothing growing up as children, which was true.

Dad was born in Jersey just six weeks before the German troops invaded the Island on 30th June 1940 during the Second World War. During the five hard years that Jersey was occupied by the Germans, they suffered many years of hardship and even following the Liberation on May 9th 1945, things were very difficult for the Islanders for a long time, especially large families like his; he was one of seven children. They did not have basic essentials and were starving. The Red Cross charity played a huge part in helping the Islanders survive during this period, with food parcels and packages and delivering communications to loved ones, I love to support this wonderful charity.

For the otoplasty operation itself, we all decided it should be done in my school holidays so that no one would be any the wiser, I checked into a private BUPA hospital in Nottingham. I remember that the operation was done under local anesthetic, I couldn't feel any pain but I could hear them working and cutting behind my ears.

When I woke up the following morning, I was in agony though. I was given some type of painkillers but I don't think they were very effective; I was in a lot of pain during the car journey home from Nottingham back to Stoke-on-Trent. I remember dashing inside to our home, I didn't want any neighbours to see my bandages! When I returned to the hospital a few days or maybe a week or so later and the bandages were removed, I was ecstatic with my new flat ears, I remember the surgeon looking pleased with his work and kindly saying as he handed me a hand mirror, "There you go, take a look in the mirror at the future Miss World." How funny.

Helen was now a successful and regular face on the beauty queen scene in Stoke-on-Trent and further afield, because the prize money and prizes were very attractive, not to mention the thrill of winning a sash and title. She invited me to go along with her and get involved. My first ever beauty contest that I entered with Helen was for one of the qualifying rounds of the Miss Stoke-on-Trent title, Miss Hanley. Hanley is the principal town in Stoke-on-Trent and therefore, the Miss Hanley beauty contest was quite competitive with lots of hopefuls.

I went along with Helen to Robateaux nightclub with my competition dress and swimsuit and high heels at the ready and we got changed and ready in the back stage dressing room area, The girls had travelled from towns all around Stoke-on-Trent to enter. I could see why Helen would have enjoyed to take me along with her, to have a friend on side. I could feel the competitive atmosphere and some of the girls were quite mean with their comments. One by one, we were called out to walk around the dance floor to music, in front of a panel of judges. First we wore our dresses and next our swimsuits. The room was packed and I felt a bit nervous, but at the same time I found it exciting and felt very grown up. We all had short interviews over the microphone asking us a few questions about ourselves. Then, the moment came when they announced the judges' results. All the girls lined up looking nervous; they announced the winners in reverse order—third, second and first. Imagine my absolute shock when I was announced as the third place winner! I walked out on to the stage in disbelief and received my sash, a bouquet of flowers, a bottle of champagne and a £100 cash prize. I simply couldn't believe it.

I never entered a Miss Stoke-on-Trent beauty competition again, but a few months later, spurred on once again by Helen, I entered a local heat of a National beauty competition, Miss Wilsons Calendar Girl, that was organized by Wilsons Brewery. In National competitions, there were *very* attractive prizes to be won. The winners could walk away with large cash sums, cars, fabulous overseas holidays and modeling contracts. For this competition as well as these prizes, the winners would feature in the Wilsons Brewery calendars in swimsuits adorning pub walls around the whole of the UK! and have the chance to do other paid modeling contracts. Everyone needed to be over 18 years to enter due to the sponsors being an alcohol related business; but no one bothered asking for any proof of our ages. I filled in the form, making myself two years older than my actual age of 16, besides I was nearly 17! There were several older girls that used to detract a few years from their ages, it was well known.

Helen and I set off to our local heat in Staffordshire at Robateaux, with our competition dresses, swimsuits and heels. This was a much larger competition; there were girls who had travelled from all over the country, since there were no rules saying that you needed to live in the county where you were competing for a title. Many of the girls did this as their full time job, travelling up and down the country competing for lucrative prizes and modeling contracts. There would be 3 winners again in each county, with the first and second place winners qualifying to go through to the National final in Manchester at a huge venue called Quaffers.

Can you believe it? Once again I won third place!

The next morning I rushed downstairs to tell Mum who was busy with my little brother that I'd won third place and received a sash, money, flowers and a free course of sun beds at a tanning salon. I was a very happy 16-year-old and thought no more of it as I headed out the door to school.

A week later though the organizers phoned to say that the first-place winner had dropped out of the final and handed back her sash since she was going on a modelling job overseas. This meant that as third place, I was now bumped up to second place and therefore competing in the National final!

The next few weeks were hectic, finding the right dress for the big final in Manchester and trying to eat nothing to look my best. Mum and Dad treated me to a beautiful long red gown, which I needed for the final heat, which was my birthday present early. I travelled up to Manchester with Mandy, the other finalist from Staffordshire who lived nearby.

We arrived at Quaffers and unpacked our dresses, heels and swimsuits and were all invited for cocktails. Then, we had to go into an individual interview with the panel of judges. I remember them asking me a few questions about how old I was and when I left school, what did I do now; I think they knew I was underage because I faltered a bit on my answers, but they let me continue anyway. Robateaux nightclub in Stoke-on-Trent who had hosted the local qualifying round, rented a mini bus and they came up to Manchester to support Mandy and me on the night, which was lovely. Neither of us won anything in the final, but it was an amazing night to be a part of. Something I'll always remember.

I couldn't wait to finish school now, I just wanted to leave and start going for auditions and see if I had what it took to get offered professional work.

I vividly remember my last day at school and after completing my final exams feeling so relieved and happy. I walked home from Blythe Bridge High school for the last time feeling as though I was floating on air and free.

Dad told me I needed to get a job immediately and start to pay rent, so I started to look for a job so that I'd be able to afford to go to auditions in London and pay my rent.

I saw an advert in the local paper for a new sun bed shop opening in Stoke-on-Trent, that'd be great I thought, free sun beds so that I'd look

14

tanned for auditions and local modeling jobs that I was doing in the meantime. I wrote in and applied for the job and was delighted when I received a call to go and attend an interview in person a few days later. I went to meet the man at the sunbed salon, it was a new building. "This is where it's going to be," he said. I could see that they were preparing rooms and there were sun beds not yet unpacked. He gestured for me to go into his office and sit down opposite him and made small talk, asking about my dancing and modeling and telling me a bit about the salon. Next he asked me to stand up, so he could "have a proper look at me." I stood up nervously and I could see him ogling me. I left the interview as quickly as possible and took the bus home. By the time I walked in the front door, he was phoning to offer me the job, but I turned it down immediately and told him I'd decided it wasn't really what I wanted to do. I heard from Mum the following year when I was dancing overseas, that the sunbed salon had been shut down because they were offering a little more than just sunbed tanning!

My next interview was at a beautiful wedding shop, Pronuptia and Young's in Hanley. This was run by a delightful husband-and-wife team—Ken ran the menswear department upstairs and Margaret his wife ran the ladies bridal wear downstairs. I was upstairs most of the time with another lady and the seamstresses who did all of the alterations. I enjoyed my first job overall and my plan was always that it should only be for a short while until I landed a dancing job. It was really interesting getting to meet all of the brides and grooms and their families getting fitted out in top hats and tails and stunning wedding dresses. I learned lots of skills, including how to steam the men's Morning suits and fold them carefully between tissue paper into suitcases ready for the big day and brush the top hats when they came back from a wedding. On the Friday, all of the men would come in to collect their suits. We would laugh and joke with them and it was generally a very nice atmosphere, charged with the excitement of a beautiful wedding. It was a big responsibility to get everyone's orders perfect for the biggest day of their lives and we were a very conscientious team and never faulted, besides Ken would have been furious if we had, he was a strict man but a fair man and he had very high standards.

Sometimes, in my lunch hour or if it wasn't too busy, Margaret would call me downstairs and ask me to try on the new wedding dresses that had arrived. I absolutely loved this. She would get me to model them for her and the other ladies in her department to see. This was definitely my favourite part of the job.

Next, Helen told me about a 6-month contract for Superkings Tobacco who wanted glamorous promotion girls at the Stoke-on-Trent National Garden festival. We both applied and were delighted to be selected. How funny nowadays to think that at a garden festival, which is something open air and healthy, the big sponsor was a cigarette brand, but it was. They employed about 15 of us for the 6 months to wear yellow-and-black striped branded outfits looking a bit like James Bond girls and walk around smiling & directing people round the garden festival and *especially* reminding them that there were cigarette kiosks on the way.

We were paid very well on this job and as part of our package we were allowed one packet of free cigarettes every day. I did not smoke at the time so I used to sell mine to one of the other girls.

The garden festival was open every day, so we were on a rota and it was quite easy to swap days off with one of the other girls, so it was perfect to be able to go to an audition. I saw one that I liked the sound of for a show in Spain and wrote off. I was over the moon when I received an invitation to go to London for the audition; I organized my day off to be able to attend in London.

The Audition That Changed My Life

I was 17-years-old and my big brother had kindly offered to drive me down to London to attend the audition that was about to change my life. On the way down to my audition, I was moaning to Adey in the car because I couldn't afford to buy myself a new leotard for the audition, on top of which, when id packed my leotard in my bag I noticed a couple of tiny holes appearing along the seam too. The older girls at my dance academy had told everyone that you really needed to look and feel your very best at auditions to stand out from all the other hundreds of girls vying for a place. Feeling good about yourself was key to being confident and dancing to the highest standard. My leotard was not exactly ideal to make me feel super confident.

I found Pineapple Dance studios where I needed to go in Langley Street, Covent Garden. Widely recognised as the foremost dance centre in the UK. It has seen some of pop's biggest musical acts rehearse their worldwide tours there, including Michael Jackson, Beyonce, Janet Jackson, Kylie Minogue and Madonna.

We had arrived in plenty of time and had a little walk around Covent Garden and headed to the undercover market area, we went down to the ground floor and found a wine bar that is still there to this day, situated right up the corner and I decided to have a glass of wine to calm my nerves.

I headed towards Langley Street and killed a little more time in the Covent Garden General store, which was very near to Pineapple Dance studios. The smell of fresh cookies was unbelievable, for many years later in dressing rooms all around the world; we dancers would all talk about the cookies at Covent Garden General Store. Sadly the store closed down but dancers from that time all remember it fondly. I think we all went in there *after* our auditions and ate fresh cookies to either celebrate our new job or commiserate if we had not been chosen.

I walked up the steps into Pineapple for the first time, noticing the dance studio on the right-hand side of the entrance that has a window where you can stand in the street and look through and see the dance class taking place. Michael Jackson once used that *exact* studio to rehearse and there were crowds of fans in the street looking through the window watching him.

I could not quite believe that I was actually here. I checked with reception and asked for directions to the studio where I would be auditioning. I wandered down to the changing rooms passing by several dance studios on the way where you could watch through the windows and see dance classes taking place, rehearsals and auditions and started to get ready with all of the other hopefuls.

There was a large changing room area with lots of benches, sinks, big mirrors, toilets and some showers for people to use. It was busy with lots of the dancers who knew each other excitedly chatting. I pulled on my tights and purple lycra leotard and hoped the small holes weren't noticeable, which to be honest they weren't. I put on my makeup and did my hair. There were so many girls who all seemed super confident and very glamorous. Everyone was trying to get a place in front of the mirror so that we could do a final check of our make-up. It was important to look and feel our very best to feel confident and dance our best. I did feel as though I was from a small village and dancing academy though compared to these other dancers hearing them talk.

Most of the dancers that I auditioned and subsequently worked with were from very prestigious full time Professional dancing colleges such as Italia Conti, Doreen Bird, Ballet Rambert, Laine Theatre Arts, Hammond School, to name a few.

Miss Veronica and Miss Susan had taught me well though and I had always worked exceptionally hard at my dancing. I was lucky to have had great teachers who gave us the training and confidence to be able to hold our own at these auditions.

As well as training, it really comes down to your own natural flair and talent. There are some people who could train all their lives and will never have what it takes to be a professional dancer.

I was desperate to get this first professional dancing job.

I made my way up to the studio and we waited outside of the door to be called in and start. I felt nervous and excited at the same time. Today at least was not like the open auditions where you simply turned up with hundreds of other hopefuls, It was by invitation only and I was delighted to have been chosen to attend the audition. It was also an Equity contract.

Equity is the UK union that represents professional performers. To become a member you needed to provide evidence that you had accrued a certain amount of months working professionally on an Equity contract or, for a company on a contract that was an affiliate and approved by Equity.

The problem was at this time, a huge proportion of jobs advertised were only open to performers who were *already* Equity members and would say EQUITY ONLY may apply. It was a sort of chicken and egg situation. There were a few contracts, like this one, that were open to non-Equity members and would count towards your membership and as a result competition for these jobs was always extremely high.

One thing that is vital to point out is that for all of these glamorous shows, the height requirement for dancers was usually always minimum 5 foot 6 inches and above depending on the show. In the advertisements for the auditions it would always clearly state the *MINIMUM HEIGHT* required. Traditionally showgirls have always been tall; in some of the Paris shows the minimum height is 5'10". The reason for this really is that our elaborate costumes, huge feather back packs and headdresses are so huge that tall dancers show off the costumes to better effect. Smaller dancers would look rather swamped in them.

There was always an understanding amongst dancers that we all lied about our heights on our CV adding an extra inch or even two. My true height was 5'6 ¼" but I used to say that I was 5'7".

Luckily, because I had curly thick hair it added extra height to my appearance and I always got away with it. Also, if you ticked all the boxes they required, then they would sometimes overlook that you were maybe obviously an inch shorter. The most important thing to be hired was to be an excellent dancer with outstanding style and personality. Often at auditions they would actually measure dancers, which never happened to me. I attended many auditions where there were dancers who were technically brilliant, but they did not ooze personality and were therefore not chosen for jobs.

Shorter dancers did not have a chance of working in any of the big extravaganza shows in Paris and Madrid or Las Vegas. I had a couple of friends who were excellent dancers and the jobs available for them to audition for, due to their height, would be West End musical theatre shows if they were good enough, summer seasons around the United Kingdom, pantomimes and cruise ship contracts. There were a few contracts also in Japan that accepted shorter dancers too.

We filed into the dance studio and all started warming up in our own chosen way, I started by doing some plies at the bar and stretching out my muscles. My heart was beating wildly, my stomach was doing somersaults and my hands were sweating due to nerves. My mind was also racing. *How difficult will the choreography be? Will I be able to pick it up quickly enough?* I was hoping and praying that I did not mess it up.

After some quick introductions by the team from Spain the audition began. I remembered Miss Veronica saying, "Get to the front where you can see and be seen," so I did just that and put myself near the front centre of the studio.

The choreographer showed us the routine and we all joined in trying to pick up the steps and moves as quickly as we could together, then they asked us to dance in groups of around 12. While the other groups were taking their turn to perform, I used this time wisely and continued to mark through the steps at the side or back of the studio until it was my turn to perform again. Each time we rotated and when it was my turn to perform with my group, I tried my best to add a little of my own flair and style into the choreography and smile from ear to ear to catch their eye. When we had all finished we were asked to stand in a row. The choreographers picked out a few of us in that group and asked us to stay, then thanked the others and said that they could go.

I was through to the next stage, this continued, with all of us dancing again and again proving ourselves to the same routine until the final selection was made and I was one of the chosen ones. I was so excited I wanted to *burst!*

The Spanish choreographer went through our CVs to check he had the right candidate's identities and paper work and told us that they would be sending our contracts and plane tickets in the post ready to start the next month. I exchanged numbers with another dancer who had been chosen on that day, a friendly, pretty, blonde girl with huge sparkling blue eyes called Beverley who had trained at the Italia Conti stage School.

I could not get changed quickly enough and ran to a bright red London phone box outside, I did not have a mobile phone. I phoned my mum, praying that she would be at home and answer the phone to tell her the good news. She picked up and I told her my exciting news. I was going to Spain as a professional dancer. I had been chosen. I got the job!

My brother Adey had been hanging around the Covent Garden area for some time waiting for me, with no mobile phones it was much harder to update one another, we would have to say, "I'll meet you here around 2 p.m.," but often things changed due to circumstances. On that day, because I had been successful at my audition, it had taken a lot longer organizing things with my soon to be new boss and choreographer Ricardo Ferante.

Thankfully Ade and I found each other at the phone box eventually and we decided that we would go for Pizza to celebrate.

We headed to the underground station at Covent Garden Station and got in the big lift which took everyone down to the platform, I was beaming from ear to ear, I felt as though I was going to burst with happiness, I kept saying out loud to Ade, "I can't believe it I'm going to Spain, I've got the job!"

I felt like telling everyone on the entire London underground train.

That was possibly the best pizza I have ever eaten in my entire life due to the happiness filling my entire body and head, although I did feel a little *teeny-weeny* bit guilty, since the new bosses had asked all the girls to please follow healthy diets and watch their weight. The beautiful costumes we were about to be dancing in for the next few months were tiny. Absolutely no room for any spare inches.

In the next few weeks before I flew out to Spain to join the company, Beverley and I spoke to each other on the phone a couple of times excitedly chatting about what we would take with us to Madrid. I ate healthily and I would jog around the field that our home backed on to, being careful to avoid cow pats. This is probably the only time I can remember jogging in my whole life because I hate it. I've wished many times that I enjoyed running and jogging but I really don't. I have joined many gyms around the world too on various dance contracts, forcing myself to do exercise that I hated and as I became wiser with age, I decided that I would only do exercise that I *enjoy*.

CHAPTER TWO

Spain

S o, at the beginning of June, very early in the morning, before it was even light, I said a tearful farewell to my Mum and Adey at Hanley bus station to get the National Express coach down to Gatwick Airport in London. Little brother Chalky was at home asleep with Dad looking after him.

I hadn't seen Dad for at least a couple weeks and last time I'd seen him we had argued about something. I honestly can't remember what about, but my father was a very difficult and domineering character. He didn't bother to see me or say Goodbye or Good luck even. In all the years that were to follow where I danced all over the world, he never came to see me in any of the shows that I appeared in, other than the Caesars Palace show in Jersey, where he grew up.

I have thought many times how sad that is. I could not imagine having a child and not making the effort to go and see and support them in these wonderful shows.

On the way down, we had to change coaches at Birmingham bus station and unfortunately our next coach had problems and was delayed. Sitting at Birmingham coach station stressed out, a girl a little older than me started talking to me, "Are you a dancer?" she asked How *weird*, I thought.

What does a dancer actually really look like? Maybe it was the way we walked. "Yes, I'm actually on my way to Spain to start a contract." Being able to say those very words gave me such a thrill, I felt so excited and proud. It transpired that she was also a dancer and was on her way back to Spain too but not on the same flight as me. Her name was Mandy and she had danced a few contracts in Spain already, she was going back to be with her Spanish boyfriend who she had met while dancing out there and then going to look for another dancing job. She asked who I was going to work for and was very impressed when I told her Ricardo Ferrante, "Wow he is the top choreographer in Spain," she told me. "He has the best shows and TV shows and pays the best money." I was delighted to hear this obviously. After some time we eventually set off from Birmingham, Mandy and I sat next to each other for the rest of the journey and chatted all the way to the airport.

I ended up being really delayed due to roadwork's on the motorway and I would have missed the plane by hours, but fortunately the plane was also very delayed by several hours and therefore I made It. In those days the gate did not close and so, if your plane was late and you were too, it worked in your favour, thank goodness.

I found the other dancer who was also flying out with me on the same flight called Erin and we sat next to each other on the plane. We both admitted that we were hungover having been out the night before for farewell drinks with our friends. What a stupid thing to do when travelling to a job the next day. We both snoozed on the plane a bit and then when I woke up, I leaned over and looked out of the window. Below me, I could see Orange groves stretching far and wide. How exciting, I really was flying over Spain and almost in Madrid. I had only ever been to France on school trips and other than that all of my family holidays had been in Jersey or the UK.

When Erin and I arrived in Madrid airport there was a male dancer who also worked for Ferrante who had been sent to meet us. He was called Alfredo, originally from Argentina like Ferrante. Thankfully, he spoke great English, because neither Erin nor I spoke a word of Spanish or had an address. Alfredo was very helpful and told us we were on our way to Calle

Santa Isabel, (calle means "street" in Spanish) which was where the dance studios were that we would be rehearsing in starting the following morning. He pointed out the dance studios Estudios Nachos. I remembered that this address was where we originally had to write in, sending our photos and CV before the audition in London. Now, here I was at that very address. The dance studios are still there in 2020 and still look exactly the same. Alfredo then pointed out in the same street a small 'pension' which is a lodging house, where the dancers were renting rooms for the next couple of weeks while we rehearsed. We went into the Pension and with the help of Alfredo translating, organized our accommodation. The little old Spanish lady showed us to our rooms, she did not have much space left. I took a single room which was absolutely tiny, with a little sink and mirror at the end and Erin agreed to share with another Australian dancer Lynda, who was already there in a room.

It was Sunday, so it was a quiet day; Alfredo walked us around the immediate neighborhood for 10 minutes or so, pointing out a bakery nearby, and teaching us a few words in Spanish. On the way back to our pension, we stopped at the stage door of a nearby theatre and he introduced us to his girlfriend Kelly who was rehearsing another group of dancers, for a different Ferrante production in Madrid. She was American and seemed very glamorous and confident.

As we walked the streets of Madrid, It was really hot and sunny and I always remember strong and significant smells, the strong smell of Tobacco, wafting through the hot air, usually "Fortuna" and "Camel" cigarettes that the locals seemed to smoke and the wonderful food smells, such as "Jamon" ham, garlic and paprika and Spanish cheese, oozing out from the local bars and cafes all around. There were always large Jamon legs hanging from the ceilings of the bars, and the floor was littered with sawdust and empty pistachio shells, until a waiter would do his sweep up, it was all part of the ambience. Even now whenever I get off the plane in Spain and experience these kinds of smells, it transports me instantly back and reminds me of this significant and exciting time in my life.

That evening Erin I went out for food with Lynda, an Australian dancer and another British dancer called Sandra. Lynda and Sandra had recently been working in another show in Spain together, so they showed us some places to eat and some little shops on the way back to get some water and snacks for the following day.

I slept well and woke up wondering where I was and then remembered Madrid! How exciting.

I ate a 'Bollycao' for breakfast, which was a bit like a French *pain chocolate*. I had taken with me a water heater, it was basically like an element from the bottom of a kettle, which you plugged into the wall and stuck it in a cup or mug of cold water to heat it up, so that you could have tea or coffee. Unfortunately it didn't work very well with the adaptor, so I gave up on that idea and drank some cold water. I showered down the hallway, pulled on my rehearsal clothes and did my makeup. Then I went across the road to Estudios Nachos to start rehearsals and meet the choreographer and the other dancers.

On the first day of rehearsals, our choreographer and boss Ricardo Ferrante was there in the studio already. He was a very well known choreographer in the world of dancing and he was quite an intimidating character too. Originally from Argentina, he had worked with great people including Bob Fosse. He was very respected and everyone was always a little scared of him, he had that kind of presence about him. Our actual day-to-day choreographer who taught us all of the routines was an exceptional dancer called Luis, also from Argentina.

I met the rest of the team of dancers from all over the world, who were arriving one by one.

There were eleven female dancers altogether in this show: Catarina from Sweden, Lynda from Australia, three from Spain, and the rest of us were British, including our dance captain, Shani, who had been living in Spain for many years.

Catarina and Miguel were two of the first dancers that I spoke to, Catarina was a tall, beautiful dancer around 5 feet 10 inches in height, of

Swedish descent. She spoke English and Spanish fluently along with a few other languages. She was super friendly and she was always genuinely kind and helpful. Miguel was her boyfriend, a tall, dark and handsome local from Madrid with a fun personality and a gorgeous smile. They became very close friends of mine and still are, we have remained in contact all of our lives.

There were two other male dancers in the show; Aldo and Mario, who at the time were also a couple. They were both from Argentina and had moved to Spain because there was more dancing work for them. Both were two of the most beautiful specimens that I have ever seen with their striking looks and bodies.

I adored Aldo and Mario; they were like big brothers to me and they treated me like a little sister. We too became great friends and remained in contact. I also had the opportunity to dance with Aldo again in Madrid a few years later in the SCALA Madrid show that I talk about later here in the book. Sadly, Mario passed away from HIV related diseases. At that time HIV was the big scary disease, like a death sentence. Now thankfully there are very good drugs available and people can control it and live long lives with the disease.

We started to warm up, I did feel nervous, but I remembered Miss Veronica's advice and placed myself at the front of the studio so that I had a good clear view of the choreographer. Rehearsals started well for me, each day I enjoyed it and felt more confident, I picked up the routines easily and loved the choreography, it was energetic and dynamic. Once the show opened and we were doing the same choreography in high heels, wigs and headdresses, it all had to be compromised, as is often the case.

After rehearsals finished for the day, myself and Beverley who I had met at the audition in London decided to try and find some better accommodation together and wandered around a few streets until we found a twin room in a pension called Al Hambra, near to Puerta del Sol. Our room was a few floors up and looked out on to the street with a tiny Juliette-style balcony. We had to go down the Corridor to use a shared bathroom and shower, but it was all spotlessly clean and very nice.

We rehearsed for hours and hours every day, which was very demanding and we were exhausted at night, but I loved the challenges and satisfaction that rehearsals presented to me.

Each day I felt like pinching myself I could not believe I was actually here on a professional dancing job getting paid money to do what I loved, dance all day.

We didn't have much money during rehearsals, since we were waiting for our first pay day.

Beverley and I found a little bar near to our accommodation where we would eat tapas occasionally, hot *patatas bravas* in spicy tomato sauce or cold *tortilla,* delicious Spanish omelette with potatoes and onions. One day, just before payday we were down to our last few *pesetas,* which was the currency in Spain before the Euro, and we chipped together for some food and were horrified when the bill came and found we were five pesetas short. By a stroke of luck, we found five pesetas glistening on the floor underneath the table.

Another night in our room, we were extremely hungry and had a couple of tins of tuna and sardines in tomato sauce, we had a really rubbish tin opener on a penknife that didn't work we found out! The most annoying thing was we had managed to pierce the tin and now we could smell the fish in tomatoes. When you are so hungry it smelt like the most amazing food ever. We fell to sleep with rumbling stomachs.

One day during rehearsals, we had a rare morning off, so Beverley and I decided that we would go to Madrid's famous park El Retiro Park and do a spot of sunbathing. El Retiro is truly beautiful to walk around, over 125 hectares and filled with interesting sculptures, fountains and a large boating lake. It was always popular with *Madrilenos* (locals from Madrid) taking a stroll and we loved how the families all still dressed up on Sundays, being predominantly a Catholic country, lots of families would dress up to go to church and then walk in the park.

We were strictly forbidden to have unsightly strap marks from sunbathing, since this would look unsightly in our beautiful costumes. Therefore, we were told by our dance captain Shani to sunbathe topless to prevent this. Beverley and I found a deserted spot in the park and laid out our towels on the grass, whipped off our bikini tops and started to bask in the hot Spanish sun. After around 15 minutes, some gardeners from the park appeared and started shouting at us and waving their arms around and pointing to the exit. They were NOT amused that we were sunbathing topless and even though they did not speak English and we did not speak Spanish, we understood very clearly that we were not welcome to sunbathe topless in the park. After quickly covering up and dressing ourselves, we walked home to our accommodation, laughing our heads off. We were honestly both a little surprised that the gardeners had not turned a blind eye; they were actually *very* angry with us.

I loved living in Madrid during this rehearsal period; I loved walking the streets taking in the sights and sounds that were so different from England. I loved how everyone sat on the pavements socialising and eating and drinking in all these bars and Cafes and watching the world go by. I even loved how the cheeky Spanish men would openly shout *"hola, guappa"* at us which basically means *"hello, gorgeous."*

It was in Madrid too that I first discovered and fell in love with El Corte Ingles, *the* most wonderful Spanish department store.

El Corte Ingles sell everything that you would expect to find in an upmarket department store, plus lots of interesting Spanish brands and products unique to Spain. The main attraction for us was really the extensive make up supplies, including false eyelashes that we needed to buy for the show. I recently have been back to El Corte Ingles stores in Barcelona and Palma and Madrid and always leave happily loaded up with bags. They always have a good restaurant, usually on the top floor and a supermarket, on the ground floor should you ever find yourself in one.

One night near the very end of our rehearsal period in Madrid, we were all invited to go to Joy Eslava for drinks with Ricardo Ferrante and the

Producer of our show Jose Ortiz. Joy Eslava is near to Puerta del Sol, a legendary nightclub in Madrid, which originally opened its doors in 1872 as a theatre and then was converted into a nightclub. It was a very plush, cool nightclub with security on the doors and it had that feeling of VIP about it, everyone looked very glam and beautiful that went there. There were lots of footballers that played for Real Madrid and Models dancers and musicians, it was full of fabulous people enjoying themselves, drinking, dancing and chatting. We all sat around with our bosses and ordered our drinks. I was 17 and had not tried lots of drinks, so I stuck to my Martini and lemonade. We were all having a great time, dressed up for once instead of wearing our rehearsal clothes, chatting and laughing.

We were not short of male attention being pretty young dancers, one of the girls was enjoying it so much that she slipped off her engagement ring and put it on her other hand on another finger. We wondered back to our table and more drinks were there for us, all paid for by the bosses, Jose the producer did not speak much English, but he asked myself and Lynda if we wanted Coke, I was thinking no thanks I'm fine with the Martini and Lemonade. He put something in Lynda's hand. Lynda grasped my hand and said, "Come to the toilet with me," nothing unusual about that, girls like to go to the toilet together, but once inside the toilets, she squealed and told me, "Oh my God he has given us Cocaine!" We were both shocked and also in hysterics. I'd never even *seen* Cocaine in my small country village, it wasn't something that was even talked about and certainly not used by anyone to my knowledge. I genuinely didn't know what you were even supposed to do with it.

We went into a cubicle together, so as not to be seen and flushed the cocaine down the toilet. When we went back out to join the party, we just smiled and hit the dance floor avoiding Jose until we went home.

At the end of our intense rehearsal period in Madrid, we were ready to go on tour with the show looking very polished. We all met at the designated area, Plaza Cibeles on the corner right near El Retiro Park and saw for the first time our tour bus.

This was basically a regular sort of coach. Everyone piled aboard, all the dancers, the actors, the wardrobe mistress and a few other people who worked behind the scenes on our show. The dancers all spread ourselves out and adopted seats which would be ours for the next few months each time we piled on the tour bus to leave one town and travel to the next town. We could sit anywhere that we wanted to on the bus and there were plenty of seats, but humans tend to be creatures of habit so we all tended to gravitate towards the same seats each journey. I had two seats to myself across the aisle from Beverley.

The smokers mostly sat at the front. I hated the smell since I did not smoke at the time, but somehow got used to it. How terrible for our health breathing in the smoke in the bus all day and night. Our tour bus journeys were often overnight, we would come off stage after the last show and all pile on to the bus, so we slept on two seats each, hurtling around Spanish roads through the night but sleeping somehow.

We were like one big family, the bonds we made were so strong, because not only did we dance together, we lived together, we ate together, and we travelled together. We talked about our lives and our families together and we basically did everything together.

Our first destination was the city of Burgos where our show opened on June 27th to a packed audience. We usually performed two shows a night at around 8.15 p.m. and 11.15 p.m. We performed there for 6 continuous nights to sell out shows and after our final performance; we boarded our tour bus at 3.30 a.m. in the morning, heading to our next city, Gijon on the northern coast of Spain.

"*Teatro*" means Theatre in Spanish and on tour our *teatro* was a huge travelling theatre. I have never to this day seen anything quite like this; it was really a huge tent with a theatre built inside, an enormous auditorium with row after row of seats, and the huge stage at the front. The team would get there in advance and assemble the theatre ready for the show. What a huge amount of work, I cant remember exactly, but I believe there were two theatres, so one team would go ahead and set up a teatro ready in the next town while the other team would stay and dismantle the *teatro* that we had just performed in and so on. There was a huge team of workers who did all of the assembly and they were mostly from Morocco. We rarely saw these men, because we would arrive at the *teatro* once it was all set up and already be on the tour bus headed for the next city before they started dismantling it.

Backstage the *teatro* had been segmented into lots of dressing rooms for us all, with thick stripy fabric curtains. I shared my dressing room with Beverley. We had mirrors surrounded with bright light bulbs and our elaborate costumes hung around on hooks and hangers.

The weirdest thing about this travelling *teatro* was that there were not any toilets, so we all had plastic buckets in our changing rooms to pee in!

I honestly thought this was a joke at first, but it was not. Before we entered the *teatro* for the show we would always find the closest café or bar to the theatre for our last chance to use a proper toilet before the show. Thereafter, once we were inside the *teatro* and the show started, if we were desperate, we had to pee in the bucket! or wait for the gap between the first show and the second show. It was actually quite hilarious, we invented a little game and if we needed to use the bucket we would shout out a pee alert and then everyone would sing "I'm singing in the rain" until the person had finished! That was the most *un*glamorous thing about being on tour in this show.

Backstage there was always lots of excited chatter as we arrived at the *teatro* and applied our make up and scraped our hair back into neat buns in hairnets, securing it with hair spray, ready to go underneath either magnificent headdresses or wigs with our costumes. We would chat about our day and swap gossip as we put our make up on.

The Art of Being a Showgirl

I had obviously used make up in my dancing school shows, but now we were required to wear and use proper showgirl make up. Our dance captain Shani told us what we should buy. Since we were on tour, we all bought small toolboxes with handles on to use as our make up caddies and I continued to do this for several years afterwards. Much better than a make up bag where everything gets all jumbled up.

I loved the whole process of transformation when applying my stage make up, it turned us all into unrecognizable beauties, it felt like we were leaving behind the every day and turning ourselves into mythical stage goddesses!

We would start with pancake foundation, usually from Max Factor or Kryolan, we wet a small sponge and applied this to our faces and blended it down on to our necks. It gave the most wonderful flawless base with which to then carry-on painting, to basically turn ourselves into beautiful looking dolls with big eyes and eyelashes and red lips.

The stage lights are so strong and bright that our make up needed to be heavy and because we are far away from the audience up on our stages, we need to accentuate our features in an over-the-top way. Our costumes were also so big and magnificent that we needed to make sure our faces were too.

Next, we would cover our base foundation in powder; this sealed the base and helped prevent any dewy perspiration appearing if we were sweating from the heat of the stage lights and any of the more strenuous dance routines. I also learned to leave a little extra pile of powder on my cheekbones, so that if any dark eye shadow fluttered on to our cheeks as we applied it, which it inevitably did, then we could brush it away with the surplus powder easily without it leaving dark streaks or blemishes on our cheeks. To this very day, whenever I'm applying eye shadow, I still use this technique, far easier than trying to remove eye shadow or add extra foundation to cover.

We favoured orangey-terracotta-coloured eye shadows on the inside of our eyes near to our noses, because this really made our eyes "pop." Especially blue eyes like mine. In the very corner nearest to our nose we would apply a little white eye pencil or shadow. Again this was all to open our eyes up and make them look huge. Then on the outer edges and sweeping up towards our brow area we would apply dark colours, usually browns with darker brown on the brow bone area to make our eyes seem larger again.

Our eyebrows we made much darker, longer and thicker to really frame our eyes and faces, just underneath our brows we would use a pale white or gold colour to highlight and accentuate that area.

The most important part of the showgirl make up process and the bit that really transformed us, was applying our beautiful false eyelashes.

Our lashes were thick and very good quality, very different to the lashes that are on sale in beauty aisles now. The lashes would last us a long time if we looked after them properly, which we did since they were quite expensive to buy.

False eyelashes should always be trimmed to fit the size of your eye, otherwise if they are too long they look awful and actually have a closing effect on your eyes.

We would apply a thin layer glue along the edge of the lashes, we all used copydex glue, it holds the lashes on brilliantly and is apparently the exact same ingredients as other eyelash glues that usually come in ridiculously small pots and are far more expensive. The copydex had a great rubbery texture once dry and just peeled off when we took off the lashes each night and a tube of it would last forever. I still use it to this day if I'm using any false eyelashes.

The trick is to then leave the glue for a few minutes to become "tacky" so that the eyelashes stick almost immediately, carefully apply the lashes as close to your natural lash line as possible.

Once properly in their position, we would then apply thick eyeliner along the line sweeping out and beneath our eyes. Occasionally we even used bottom lashes for even bigger, better eyes.

We always applied lots of blusher to contour and make our cheekbones stand out and then finally our lips.

The lipstick was the finishing touch, first draw beautiful big lines around your lips or generally outside and slightly bigger and then fill in with a beautiful red lipstick, a bright and glamorous shade of red.

Voila! The transformation would be complete. The whole process took us around 20 minutes; since we were doing it every night, we became experts.

Dancers fishnet tights deserve a whole section to themselves because these things are like the secret weapon of dancers. The fishnets that we used to dance in were nude-coloured and elasticated, sort of like a pair of Spanx, but for legs and were made either by Capezio or Danskin. They are made up of hundreds of tiny elasticated zigzags that are connected and pull everything in tightly and support our legs so that there is no jiggling or wobbling. There is no sheen to these tights, so they blend into the skin tone and it appeared as though we had flawless legs. They were hard wearing too, often they would catch on rhinestones or zips in quick changes, but were strong enough not to rip usually but sometimes they did. Learning to sew and repair dancers fishnets was an art in itself and one that I needed to learn immediately. I took pride in repairing my fishnets. We always used to cut off the waistband of the tights, so that the tights blended in seamlessly underneath our costumes. We would roll down the rest of the top section of the tights and use a kirby grip to secure them and tuck them into our small G-strings at the front and back so that they were not seen.

Our costumes for this show were magnificent, everything was brand new with no expense spared, and made specially to measure for each of us fitting perfectly. Since this was my first professional dancing job I (wrongly) assumed that it would always be like this, but in fact it hardly ever is. Most of the time as dancers we would wear costumes that had been worn by lots of other dancers previously, In future shows I used to quite enjoy looking at all of the other names of girls that had previously worn my costumes and wondered who would see the name 'Gaynor' in the future in their costumes around the world.

Once our hair and make up was ready and our fishnets were on, we warmed up our bodies and muscles, doing our exercises on the stage behind the curtain. Beverley and I found little gaps backstage in the wings, where we could peek out through the curtains and see the audience chatting animatedly, waiting in suspense for the show to begin. It was the end of June and so it was always very hot in the *teatro,* we could see hundreds of

Spanish ladies fanning themselves, Spanish ladies really do carry and use their fans and they are not just tourist gimmicks.

The stage hands, all dressed in dark coloured clothing, would charge around busily preparing everything and give us countdown calls, like 15 minutes, 5 minutes, at which point we would put on our shoes tightening the straps as much as possible, do our final checks in the mirror and then quickly secure our headdresses with hairpins before a bell would ring signaling for us that it was showtime and to take our positions on the stage.

The backstage lights would dim and we would all take our positions and stand silently on a mirrored staircase, waiting for the curtains to open. The thrill of standing behind the curtain was like nothing else; there was always a huge sense of anticipation from both the audience and ourselves.

As the music started and the curtain opened revealing beautifully poised showgirls standing elegantly on the staircase, you could hear the audience gasp and they would burst into applause.

Showgirls always have an air of breathtaking beauty and mystique. They represent something that is slightly aloof and untouchable. For our opening costume, we were dripping in jewels, wearing stunning silver bikinis paired with silver gloves and feather boas, topped off with huge white feather headdresses, sort of in the shape of a mushroom.

Showgirl choreography is always very graceful and elegant; all those years of ballet training come in useful. The style is graceful and sensuously seductive, with crossed thighs and elegant and feminine positioning. *Definitely* no open crotch positions in feather showgirl routines.

The walking sections are always very regal and refined, with gentle swaying of the hips in a smooth, gliding motion. Remember, while we are doing these routines, we also need to balance the heavy headdresses and backpacks and we wear high heels, but we must make this all look easy and our faces must be smiling and alluring. It is an absolute art.

In recent years, the term 'showgirl' has been hijacked and used by strippers, lap dancers and burlesque dancers. Dancers whose performances include simulating sex, stripping or raunchy choreography are not classical showgirls, it is entirely different.

Showgirls elicit desire, they provide glamour and showcase their beauty, but are deemed **unattainable.**

We would glide elegantly down the staircase and across the stage in our fabulous costumes, pirouetting, high kicking and smiling and then make a beautiful line up either side of the big staircase where the two stars of the show, Andres Pajares and Fernando Estesso would walk out and make their first entrance.

At this point, the audience would erupt into applause, cheering and standing up clapping and we would all burst into song, singing along to the backing track in Spanish,

"Hola amigos, bienvenidos! Un saludo, que tal que tal?" which roughly translates as:

"Hello friends, welcome! Best Wishes, how are you?"

Andres Pajares and Fernando Estesso were huge 'A' list celebrities and very famous in Spain. They were famous as both comedians and actors in Spain, having starred in many award-winning movies.

When people found out that we were the *'ballet'* as the company dancers are called in Spain, from the Estesso and Pajares show we were treated like royalty everywhere that we went, which of course we loved.

The format of the show was comedy sketches, starring Andres and Fernando along with a few other supporting actors, then either us dancing, or one of the world class 'Attractions' as they are known, performing in between the sketches, while sets and costumes were hurriedly changed.

The attractions we had performing with us were excellent, the attractions would spend their lives going from contract to contract all around the world performing in big shows, many had learned their skills originally from circus families and it was passed down from one generation to the next.

El Gran Picaso as he was known on stage, was an amazing artist from Valencia. His act involved him juggling ping-pong balls from his mouth and keeping five aloft at the same time. There have been many other acts that have since copied this idea, but he was known to be the original guy that invented the ping-pong ball juggling technique. He had worked all over the world and had been booked for long residences at the MGM Hotel in Las Vegas. Picaso could always be found standing backstage blowing his Ping-Pong balls up into the air and catch them in his mouth, warming up for his act. He spoke excellent English and was a friendly, charming man. One night we were just about to run on stage and he lost one of his ping-pong balls, we were all looking around frantically on the floor for it, but couldn't see it anywhere. For this routine we wore white basques underneath baby pink chiffon, marabou feather trimmed capes and long white wigs. As we all ran on to the stage the missing ping-pong ball bounced and rolled across the stage, it had been stuck to the feathers on one of our capes! We all thought this was very funny and had to try and dodge the ball and not slip or stand on it, a twisted ankle would put us out of the show and cause chaos having to re-choreograph last minute.

The Fredianis were the other act, they were three fiery Italian brothers who were incredible acrobats and they performed all sorts of daring stunts, balancing on top of one another and juggling with chairs and sometimes with one of them sat on the chair, throwing each other into the air and catching each other. They would rehearse for long hours each day perfecting their routine.

We had an impressive routine where the stage set was a circus ring and we were all dressed as tigers with myself chosen to be the Panther in the middle dressed in a black leotard. We all wore sheer leotards that were quite transparent, titillating the audiences as I liked to think of it! Aldo was dressed as a 'camp' ringmaster, dressed in gold Lycra trousers and gold knee length boots, with a bare chest strutting around the stage cracking his whip at us.

There was a high-energy tap-dancing routine with Bob Fosse style choreography that I loved, with lots of *"Do wah do wah do wah do wah!"* singing.

In between our routines, if it was not a quick change everyone would sit around in tiny flesh coloured G-strings under fishnets tights and our show heels, with just a loose t-shirt or robe, chatting and smoking. Sometimes we would all sit one behind the other on the floor with our legs in a v shape and massage the shoulders of the dancer in front, and then the person at the back would shout *"change!"* Then the person at the front would run around to the back of the shoulder massage train and so on.

Our finale costumes were absolutely spectacular. We had huge, royal blue and white circular feather backpacks, a magnificent wheel of feathers on our backs, with enormous diamante headdresses. These were very large and heavy, which obviously restricted our choreography. It was impossible to do more than glide and walk elegantly, like beautiful goddesses always smiling from ear to ear. Our bikinis were made entirely of shimmering rhinestones. On our arms we had lots more feathers that moved and flowed with us as we strutted around the stage before forming a showgirl line up and taking our final bow to rapturous applause.

Each time we arrived in a city we had to find accommodation to stay in for however many nights the show was there for. This was anything between 1 night or up to a week. Throughout the summer lots of the cities were celebrating with their *Feria*. This is an annual local festival like a carnival, so accommodation was often busy and booked up in advance. People in Spain love to celebrate and make the most of their *Ferias*. Luckily, Shani had toured Spain before and knew of 'Pensions 'and Hotels, so she would sometimes try to phone ahead and book rooms for those who wanted them. Otherwise, if that had not been possible, we simply asked taxi drivers in our limited Spanish language to take us to one. I usually shared a twin room with Beverley and all of the dancers tried to stay in the same place. There was not always enough rooms, so inevitably we ended up in different accommodation sometimes. When we could though, it was such fun all being in the same hotel together, we were like one big crazy family and had great fun popping in and out of each other's' rooms. There was always lots of partying and talking late into the night, or more accurately the early hours of the morning. Its impossible to sleep straight after a show, we always needed a period to wind down.

In one town we found the most amazing accommodation and stayed in a large room that had 13 beds in! It was the best fun; we all jumped around the room from one bed to the next doing a sort of trampoline train behind each other and then changed directions and jumped back the other way until we could bounce no more.

In the daytime we always slept late obviously and we would relax in our rooms, colour each other's hair, paint our nails, put facemasks on and go out for food or shopping. In Avila, I decided that I wanted to dye my hair blonde, for the first time ever, so I took the plunge. It really was a fun and carefree time and we were earning exceptionally good money at the time so we could afford to shop and eat out without worrying.

When we got to the town of Santander, Beverly and I decided that it would be a good idea to splash out and stay in a nice hotel. We decided that we would treat ourselves for a couple of nights of 5 star luxury. As we were checking in to the hotel, we bumped into Andres and Fernando in reception; they were also staying at the same hotel. They looked so shocked to see us, they knew that the dancers did not usually splash out on expensive hotels, but we were paid very well and could easily afford it. They started laughing and said that we were obviously ladies that had good taste. Most of the other dancers were focused on saving as much money as they could. This is obviously a good idea and also as dancers, we usually never really knew at the end of one contract when our next job would start, or how long we would have to live off our savings for. Since this was my first professional dancing job, I hadn't really learned that yet and I behaved as if I were on one big, fabulous holiday, shopping for myself and family and regular salon appointments. In the evening, Beverley and I would head to the *teatro* together, sometimes grabbing a gin and tonic on the way and stopping at a phone box to call our mums and tell them our news.

As I would see on many dancing contracts over the few next years, it was quite rare that a long-distance relationship would survive for very long.

There were many romances that happened on the tour within our company. When you are living and working and travelling around together in a small tight group, for months on end, its easy and natural that you can become attached and attracted to people. Often these can be people that you would not ordinarily choose.

I developed a crush on Andres, one of the comedians in the show. He was always really sweet and kind to me and when it was my birthday at the stroke of midnight, he organised a birthday cake to be in my dressing room for when I arrived off stage.

One of the most memorable cities that we performed in was Pamplona. In Pamplona, their fiesta is called the fiesta of San Fermin, which honours the cities patron saint, Saint Fermin. The fiesta lasts for a week, during which time people are dancing, singing and drinking in the streets all night long. Our show times were 11.15 p.m., 2.30.a.m., and even a show starting at 4.30 a.m.!

The San Fermin tradition is to wear white clothing and red waistbands and neckerchiefs. Beverley and I decided we would get into the tradition and decked ourselves out in red and white outfits and hit the streets with Aldo and Mario. It is a great atmosphere with the oldest and youngest people enjoying the fiesta. The climax of the fiesta, which it is known for worldwide, is the running of the bulls.

"Running of the bull" is where 6–10 bulls are let loose to run through the towns streets that have been cordoned off especially for the bulls to run through. Spectators all line the streets and are crammed on to every balcony or peering through any window where they can manage to get a view of the angry bulls running wildly through the streets. During this run there are always young men who want to show off their bravery, although I would say stupidity and risk their lives by running in front of the bulls. Every year around 50–100 people are injured during the run and sometimes they are gored to death by the bulls.

I had the privilege to travel and learn about many things during my dancing career, but I didn't always like everything that I experienced in different countries and cultures. The running of the bulls was one of those.

It makes me very sad that this is still allowed to happen. The poor bulls are panicking as they run along the streets, with people screaming around them. Each of these poor bulls will then end up in the bullring and be dead in a few hours. I only ever went to one bullfight in Spain and I did not enjoy it.

I personally think that bullfights are cruel and should be banned.

Every time we arrived in a town for the *feria* a touring fair and circus also arrived at the same time. We got to know some of the performers from the circus and they became our friends too, we would often bump into them in restaurants and bars after our respective shows had finished. They never stayed in the accommodation with us because they all toured with their caravans and lived in them. One of the dancers, started to date a guy called Chochi who was a clown from the circus. I often chuckled to myself imagining her parent's reaction when she told them that she had met a nice guy: "Oh that's great darling, what's his name and what does he do?" "Actually his name is Chochi, he is a clown at the circus." Not your average job! Not that there was anything wrong with being a clown, it just was unusual, but everything about our lives was pretty unusual in a great way. I loved it.

I was literally living the dream and it was hard to believe that 12 months ago I had still been at school sitting my final exams and wearing school uniform.

Since we were always on tour and changing our accommodation every few days, we never really unpacked properly, we were constantly living out of our suitcases, which for Beverley and me were getting heavier and heavier by the week as we gathered souvenirs from all of the places that we performed in and shopped in.

The suitcases were not the only things that were getting heavier, fully immersing myself into trying all of the delicious new Spanish foods and drinks, I was also getting a little heavier. Once the show finished, we would quickly remove our beautiful huge show eyelashes and fishnet tights and make our way out of the *teatro*. We would usually congregate nearby somewhere for *bocadillos, chocolate and churros,* Spanish omelette and other delicious foods, all of which are delicious but not good for the waistline!

I started spending more time with Marta, who was the leading lady actress in the show, a Spanish girl who had a great sense of humour and Andresito, the son of Andres Pajares the comedian.

Andresito was really kind, intelligent and fantastic company, he spoke perfect English having studied in the USA for a while and he and I are still friends to this day. My Spanish was improving by the day and I loved learning, so hanging out with these Spanish friends really helped me too.

My 18th birthday was approaching and we were going to be performing in Logrono on the day, which is in the Rioja wine region.

On my birthday, Beverley said that she had booked a special lunch for the two of us. We went downstairs to the restaurant in our Hotel; we had chosen a decent Hotel since I was to be celebrating my birthday there. It was such a lovely surprise when I walked in to find that all of my dearest friends from the show were there to surprise me. I really did not expect that and it was a wonderful surprise that Beverley had organized for me.

Whenever I drink Rioja wine, I always think how lucky I was to celebrate my 18th birthday there. One of the things about Rioja wine that I have always remembered is their local drink called *calimocho*, which consists of red wine mixed with coca cola. It was originally called *Rioja Libre.* It consists of equal parts of cola and red wine served over lots of ice. Sounds terrible but honestly, I can tell you it is surprisingly refreshing and good, try one!

Our tour was coming to an end and our last city to perform in was Zaragoza, where we arrived on October the 2nd.

All of the shows were as usual completely sold out. This was the hometown of Fernando Estesso so he was treated like a God here.

It was our final few shows, which gave everyone an added extra surge of energy, not that we lacked it. Doing the same show twice nightly for months of end can become repetitive and quite mentally challenging at times, but no two performances are ever the same and as performers its important to always remember that for the audience it is their first time to see the show, they have paid their money and it must be 100 % every time.

Zaragoza is a large city. It had great shops including my favourite department store, El Corte Ingles. The weather was changing, which gave us the excuse to go and buy some jumpers and winter clothes.

On our last night we were all charged with emotion. As is tradition on the last nights of shows, there were lots of practical jokes played both on stage and backstage. We glided on to the stage together for the last time in our stunning blue and white finale feathers.

As we took our final bow on stage, I remember hearing the explosion of fireworks for the last night of the Fiesta in Zaragoza, it was a fitting and spectacular ending.

Backstage, we said tearful goodbyes. Not knowing if we would ever meet again.

For those of us who had chosen to go back to Madrid, we sat quietly on our last coach journey on the way back to Madrid. Everyone reflecting in his or her own way. I think we all knew that this was the end of a very special chapter in our lives.

Second Spanish Tour

Instead of heading back to the UK I had decided that I wanted to stay in Spain and look for dancing work. Marta had invited me to go and stay at her mum's house in Madrid while I tried to find another job. Unbeknownst to me, my Mum had planned a surprise 18th birthday party for me for when I was supposed to arrive home and invited friends. Since she had already paid for food and a DJ, they all went ahead anyway and made the most and had a fun night without me!

Luck was on my side and within a few weeks, I attended an audition for the *Zori y Santos* shows that Marta's sister Loretta, another actress and singer was appearing in. I was auditioning back at Nachos studios with another well-known Spanish choreographer called Nacho Arrieta. I was offered the job and started rehearsals the very next day; Nacho was very laid back and friendly and liked to smoke marijuana in the studio on our lunch break! I rehearsed for one day only and then sent to join the show in Alicante. "The rest of the choreography they will teach you once you get there," Nacho told me, since they were already on tour and one dancer needed to leave. This time we were touring and performing in beautiful old historic theatres mostly in the South of Spain.

I arrived in Alicante on November 5th and went straight to rehearsals, I met the dance captain, this time a much older male dancer called Manolo and the girl who I was replacing, which *unbelievably* turned out to be Mandy! The very girl that I had met on the coach to London on my first job. What a coincidence. I was so happy to see Mandy, she told me that apart from herself, there was only one other English dancer called Becky, the rest of the ballet were all Spanish.

The atmosphere was so different from the Estesso Pajares show; the choreography was dated and uninspiring. Of course, not everyone is going to have the same opinion about whether choreography is good or bad, its all a matter of opinion, but there was no wow factor in this choreography at all. The costumes were ancient and tatty and smelt musty from dancers sweat; the feathers were thin and balding. The dancers were mostly Spanish in this show and I found them mean, unfriendly, and unhelpful. The principal dancer, Mari, was very ignorant and unwelcoming to me and even though my Spanish was limited I could tell that all the other dancers were afraid of her. Becky the only other English dancer was lovely, she was in a relationship with one of the Spanish Stagehands on the tour and spoke fluent Spanish. Since it was now Spanish dancers other than Becky and myself, the language was only Spanish and I needed to learn more fast!

Luckily, Marta's sister Loretta asked if I wanted to share a room with her and Victoria, another Spanish actress. The good thing about sharing a room with Loretta and Victoria was that it forced me to really improve my Spanish a lot more; they didn't speak much English at all. The three of us had so much fun together, even though we didn't speak each other's languages very fluently, that's also what made it so funny a lot of the time, when things got lost in translation. They were such lovely, friendly girls and together the three of us laughed until we cried at the bizarreness of some of the happenings on this tour.

We ended the tour in Malaga and were about to leave for Madrid. Myself, Loretta and Victoria had time for dinner first and found a Chinese restaurant and all ordered spring rolls and a few other dishes to follow. Something went horribly wrong, because once we got on the tour bus for our final journey back to Madrid, the three of us all started to feel unwell. Suddenly, Victoria yelled frantically at the bus driver to stop the bus and I too knew that I needed to get off the bus, we ran to the back of the bus and lets just say we were so glad it was night time so that the others on the bus couldn't see us through the window eliminating the Chinese food from both ends.

Unlike the Estesso and Pajares tour I did not feel sad other than saying Goodbye to Loretta and Victoria. I was excited to get back home to the UK and see my family and Christmas was approaching.

It was great to get home to Clipsham, the family home in Stoke-on-Trent at that time. Mum was so pleased to have me home and I was very happy to be reunited with my two dear brothers. Dad was pleased to see me and our fallout seemed long forgotten. Everyone was excited to hear all about my adventures and we were all excited to put the Christmas tree up.

The New Year soon rolled around and I was getting itchy feet to go off and do my next dancing job, every week I would grab The Stage newspaper and scour it, hoping for auditions.

**TWEEDALES DANCING ACADEMY, STOKE-ON-TRENT
(THIRD FROM RIGHT, STANDING)**

NATIONAL GARDEN FESTIVAL, STOKE-ON-TRENT, PROMOTION GIRL

REHEARSALS IN MADRID, *ESTESSO & PAJARES* TOUR

MY 18TH BIRTHDAY BACKSTAGE ON TOUR,
WITH FRESHLY DYED BLONDE HAIR!

FINALE COSTUME ON TOUR (FAR LEFT)

CHAPTER THREE

Escape From Italy

T hen, as luck would have it (or so I thought at the time) Erin called me to say she had been offered a job in Italy, in the city of Turin. Also, she told me excitedly that on her recommendation, having seen my photos from the Estesso Pajares show, they had offered me the job too.

Perfect, I was so excited and a few days later we headed off from Gatwick airport together again on our way to a very cold Italy.

Turin, or *Torino* as it is called In Italian, is a wealthy Italian city, known for industry, fashion and the arts. The 17th century buildings are surrounded by snow capped mountains, it is known as being the capital of the Alps region.

We arrived in Turin and were met at the airport by the boss man in an overcoat and a flat cap. I can't recall his name, so I shall refer to him as "Flatcap" since he always wore one. He took us to his apartment in Turin where he lived with his wife, who didn't speak English. He asked for our passports and put them in his office, we assumed to start organizing our work visas.

It was quite late, so we unpacked a few things in our bedroom and fell into bed tired and awoke early the next morning ready to head to the showroom and begin rehearsals.

The next morning, we walked with Flatcap through the town, we passed a cute little Italian street market selling all sorts of food and flowers, I remember thinking how lovely it would be to come here to shop for fresh fruits once we were settled into Italian life.

We turned off into a side street. "Here we are," he announced, I looked at the entrance and thought it looked quite shoddy, but often show venues can look very shoddy in the daytime and once night time falls and everything is lit up with neon lights it takes on a whole new atmosphere. "Don't judge a book by its cover," I thought. Well, suffice to say, the cover was better than the inside.

When we got inside Erin and I couldn't believe it, this was no more than a run down nightclub. There was no stage, just a dance floor where we were expected to perform our dance routines with a small area behind where there was band equipment set up, obviously no one was here during the daytime, only us for rehearsals. He immediately steered us over to the bar area, "When you are not dancing, change into your cocktail dresses and mingle at the bar here," he said, "until someone invites you for a drink, at which point you will accept and go and sit and drink with them. We only serve champagne. Once you have finished the glass of champagne, if they haven't bought a bottle, then get up and leave the table. Remember though if they do buy a bottle, you stay there, you can't afford to get drunk, so when they are not looking pour it into the plant pots around the room without them seeing or spill some under the table. Also go to the bathroom with your drink and pour it away. You will be paid a percentage commission for the drinks."

I was absolutely stunned and scared; *oh my God,* I thought, *what is this place?*

Erin and I didn't know what to say or do; we did nothing at this stage, reminding me of how young and inexperienced we were. When we had the opportunity to go to the bathroom together we whispered to each other, how on earth had we ended up here in this nightmare situation? We were afraid that if we said we didn't want to do the drinking with the clients he would be angry with us, because evidently this was how they operated and made their money. The dancing and show was an afterthought thrown in. We weren't really dancers here just pretty girls to entertain clients and part them of their money with a bit of dancing thrown in. This was not what we had trained to do.

It got worse, not only was there no stage, there was no choreographer or other dancers. We were the dancers, just us two. "You'll choreograph your own dance routines together and there are costumes and things you can use backstage. You will dance three times during the night, the rest of the time you will mingle," he said. 'Backstage' turned out to be a corridor up a few stairs, with all sorts of little cubicles, the size of small fitting rooms in shops when you want to try clothes on.

An Asian looking girl appeared from 'backstage' and told us that she was a hostess. Unlike us, the hostesses were not performers, their sole job was to mingle with the guests and get them to buy as many bottles of champagne as possible. This was how they made their money from commission only.

"This is one of the hostesses," Flatcap said. "She will show you backstage." She looked tired and matter of fact. "This is the area where you dancers can change," she said, pointing to a large cubicle area with tatty dresses and cheap looking lingerie that was intended as our 'costumes.'

Flatcap told us to start choreographing a dance routine while he sat and chatted with a couple of waiters who had come into restock shelves and clean the bar area. It's all a bit blurry, but I recall us half heartedly going through the motions of making up a dance routine. This was a nightmare.

We headed back to the apartment for an afternoon break and Flatcap told us that we would go back in the evening to start work. "But we haven't organized any routines yet," we said. "You will just be drinking and socialising tonight with clients," he said, "Be sure to wear glamorous dresses, make-up and heels."

Back in our room, Erin and I were whispering frantically to one another. What the hell is this place? What have we walked in to? How on earth are we going to get out? We told Flatcap that we were going out for a walk to phone our families and let them know we were OK and we rushed to buy phone cards and find phone boxes. I called Mum and told her a few details, I didn't want to worry her too much, but she needed to know that all was not good.

Erin fortunately had a very good friend, who happened to be from Turin. Her Mum was going to try and make contact with the family, we needed to call back a few hours later after we finished 'work' whatever the hell that was going to be.

We arrived at the club looking glamourous, looking back I wish I had made no effort and looked ugly, but Flatcap would have smelled a rat and we decided we needed to play along as if all was OK.

We went into the club, the band was playing and there were groups of men drinking at the bar and at tables, some getting up to dance with the hostesses when they felt like it.

"Right," said Flatcap "Stand at the bar and wait for someone to approach you, then, in between drinks you can get up and dance around a bit." I wanted to scream, I had not spent years and years of commitment and training to do this. Within minutes some older Italian guys in suits approached us asking us to join them for drinks. We went and sat at a table that they chose, near to the dance floor, I looked at the seating and tried to choose the best seat next to the plant so that I could tip my drink away. In all honesty these two men actually seemed very respectable and didn't want anything from us other than some polite chitchat and our attention. After an hour or so, they thanked us for our company, said, "Ciao," and left. Flatcap, who was watching us like a hawk from the end of the bar, sent one of the hostesses over to tell us to now get on the dance floor and dance a bit to the band, so we did. It also gave us chance to chat together about the situation and how we needed to get away. "We need to get our passports back," I said and Erin agreed, "When we get home one of us must distract them and the other one sneak into his office and get them."

One waiter came over and told us that we had been requested to accompany four other men for drinks. We introduced ourselves and sat with them while they ordered bottles of Champagne. Erin was better than me at chitchat and maybe because she was a couple of years older than me she was more confident. I was polite but didn't say too much. They all seemed to speak fairly good English, which was fortunate since we didn't speak Italian, but in all honestly it would have been a good excuse not to have to converse much if they hadn't. These men seemed to just want to show off and impress their clients who they were entertaining. After the initial chitchat they pretty much ignored us, chatting between themselves about business. I was terrified that they would notice that we were discreetly tipping our drinks away, but they didn't seem to thankfully.

There were lots of hostesses drinking with clients, some of the men were vile, we could see them pawing the hostesses and being very touchy feely, but that seemed to be allowed with hostesses and it appeared that they assumed that they had the right to do that, as if the hostesses were included with the purchase of their bottle of champagne. I hated it.

I felt desperately sorry for the hostesses, how had they ended up here doing this as a job?

"OK, That's enough for tonight," said Flatcap, lets go home. We drove the short distance back to his apartment in the dark night and went inside. Once inside we took off our glam clothes and heels and changed into our dancers clothes, tracksuits and trainers. He and his wife were always sat in the lounge with the TV on blaring away. They could see if we went to the front door, because we needed to walk past their lounge. "We are just going to the phone box before bed," we said, he nodded and we went out and ran to the phone box.

Erin spoke urgently to her mum, going through the details and clarifying our address Erin's Mum told us it was all arranged and the family of Erin's friend was coming to rescue us. We were to be ready with our suitcases packed. We were so lucky that our bedroom was on the ground floor and had a window that overlooked the street. Erin had already explained that we could climb out of our bedroom window; since there was no way that we could get past the lounge with our suitcases without being seen and heard.

We went back to the apartment quickly and now we just needed to get our passports.

His office was directly opposite our bedroom and luckily the door was ajar. Flatcap and his wife were still in the lounge watching TV. Erin sneaked into the office and I stood on guard by our bedroom door, so that if they stood up then I would go straight into their lounge and start talking to him to distract him, making up some rubbish questions about the next day's rehearsals, what we should wear and how long our dance routines needed to be, anything really just to keep him talking and in the lounge so that he did not notice Erin in the office looking for our passports.

Luck was on our side, neither of them moved and Erin found our passports in the top drawer of his desk and tiptoed back into our bedroom with them, and we closed our door loudly, so that they would hear and think we had gone to sleep.

We hurriedly packed our last few things into our suitcases and looked out of the window waiting for our rescuer. Within around 20 minutes we saw a youngish man pull up outside of the apartment, he waved to us and we waved back and opened the window, which slid upwards. We passed our suitcases through the window to him; they must have been fairly heavy, because we had packed for an eight-month contract. The second suitcase did make a bit of a thud as it dropped to the floor.

He put them quickly in his car boot and then Erin and I jumped through the window down to the street and quickly got into the back of his car as our rescuer jumped in the front and locked the doors, as he did so, we saw Flatcap come running out on to the street, he must have heard the noise of the suitcase dropping to the ground and spotted us in the car that had now started up its engine and came running towards the car banging on the window shouting at us "Where are you going? I bought you plane tickets, you work for me!"

I have never felt so afraid in my life. My heart was pounding in my chest and I felt like I couldn't breathe.

Our rescuer stayed calm and drove quickly away, I think it was the uncle or an older brother of Erin's friend, I cant be entirely sure I'd guess he was around 35 years old. We drove around 10 minutes away to his family apartment. Inside it was like another world, a true traditional Italian home, with a lovely cozy kitchen with a red check tablecloth like you see in Italian restaurants. The family was so kind and welcoming to us. Feeding us delicious Italian food and having made up two beds for us in a room. I still felt scared almost expecting Flatcap to come and find us and be banging on the door, which of course did not happen.

The following day we were going to get the overnight train to Paris and then continue back to England on the train. This was fairly expensive and neither of us had enough money for the total cost of these tickets, we had thought that we were going to be working and earning money, but obviously that did not work out. The Italian family kindly bought us the tickets and when we were back in the UK we transferred the money back to them. How kind these strangers were to us.

So, the following day when we awoke, the family asked us if we would like to see a little of Turin before we left that night on the train. They didn't want our only experience and memories to be about the seedy nightclub and Flatcap.

We had a lovely day sightseeing, they took us to see Juventus football ground, there was no match, but it was a spectacular stadium. We ate some more great Italian food, I still felt nervous I was still looking over my shoulder expecting Flatcap to be chasing us.

Nighttime fell and they took us to the train station, I was still feeling on edge, expecting Flatcap to come running down the platform and demand that we stay and work for him in his seedy club. We said a final, grateful thank you and farewell to our rescuers and boarded the night train to Paris.

The train was not too busy fortunately and we were lucky to find a nice carriage compartment to ourselves, old style like in old movies with two benches facing across from each other. The journey took around 7 hours, so this was great we would be able to lie down and sleep on a bench each. We chatted for a while, we finally felt relieved that we were on our way back home. We just couldn't believe what had happened to us in the last few days. What a nightmare this had turned out to be compared to our first job in Spain. During the conversation I asked Erin, "Where exactly did you hear about that job?" "In *The Stage*," said Erin, I was confused, I bought and read *The Stage* every week, as did every dancer, it was our lifeline and main source for work. "That's weird I did not see the advert," I commented. "It was in the back in the small ads," said Erin.

I'm SURE the colour must have drained from my face.

Everyone knew that you didn't go for *those* jobs, the jobs advertised in the small ads.

Everyone knew those were "dodgy" jobs for, strippers or hostesses that couldn't really dance and weren't needed to!

As we crossed the Italian French border, police came into the carriages asking to see everyone's passports, a routine check but somehow it seemed rather scary in the middle of the night.

The border policeman seemed quite pleasantly surprised that there were two pretty young girls in there and he decided to stay in our cabin and chat, I was so tired I just curled up on my side of the bed and went to sleep, but Erin flirted and chatted with him the whole night really until we got off in Paris, I suppose it relieved the boredom for both of them and passed the time. Early in the morning, our train arrived in Paris at Gare De Lyon. We now needed to get to the other station, Gare De Nord that would take around 20 minutes to get to in a taxi and was on the other side of Paris, where our train to UK would leave.

We didn't even have any French francs so we got in the taxi told him where we needed to go. When we got out at the other end, we just grabbed our suitcases out of the boot of the taxi and then gave him all the Italian

Lira that we had and said *'sorry'* several times while rushing inside. He was waving his arms around, swearing at us angrily because we didn't have French francs, which was the currency in France before Euros.

We felt a bit bad, but when you are in survival mode, you do what you have to. At least we gave him some money, which he could exchange.

We sat around Gare De Nord station for a few hours waiting for our train to London. I remember It was freezing cold and we were shivering on the platform waiting for our train, we actually found one of those air vents where warm air came up from and sat near to that to try and keep warm. I had no French francs and needed to save what little was left of my English money to buy a train ticket back to Stoke-on-Trent once I got back to London.

We bought a hot cup of tea each and we shared a cheese and ham sandwich. We were so happy when we got on the train heading back home to London.

We hugged and said our farewells when we arrived in London.

I never saw Erin again and despite looking for her on line, I have never been able to find her. It's harder sometimes with girls, because when we marry our name changes.

CHAPTER FOUR

Paris

MY ADDRESS

8 Rue de Paradis, 75010, Paris

ow funny then that a few months later I should be on my way to
my next contract back to Paris.

I had been invited to audition for the Paris contract by a London
agent, a lady called Hazel.

The show we were auditioning for was La Nouvelle Eve, one of the
oldest and most elegant revue Theatres in Paris.

La Nouvelle Eve – 25 Rue Pierre Fontaine, 75009, Paris

Built in 1898, situated at the foothills of Montmartre, La Nouvelle
Eve is a dazzling high-energy blend of music hall and cabaret featuring the
most wonderful French cancan. King Edward VIII, who was later titled
The Duke of Windsor, was a regular visitor to La Nouvelle Eve when he
lived in Paris with his wife, Wallis Simpson after he abdicated.

It was taken over by the new owners and our bosses, the Pierini brothers in 1966 and they decided to put on typically Parisian revues, the staging of which was entrusted to Georges Lugosi and Luis Diaz.

We were back at Pineapple dance studios. It was a small audition this time, with only girls that had been invited by Hazel. We were in one of the studios near to the changing rooms with large windows and people could walk past and see inside and watch the audition taking place, there were always a few curious dancers watching.

I did my best not be too nervous and think of the audition as a mini performance. Thankfully, the audition went well for me and the success-ful dancers were lined up at the end of the audition and offered the job, the great thing was that this was also an Equity contract so it contributed towards me gaining my equity card. I was ecstatic and travelled home from London with a huge sense of relief.

I went back to Stoke-on-Trent for the 4 weeks and made the most, enjoying time with my family and friends and the excitement of being able to tell people who asked, that I had been offered the contract and was on my way to Paris. Mum contacted her friend that worked as a journalist at the local newspaper and they did an article about me. Every time I took a new dancing contract now, they used to fill up half a page with a photo and details about my dancing career. It was an easy way to help fill their paper with a *local-girl-does-good* type of story. I thought back to a few mean and nasty girls from school, who used to ridicule my dreams of being a dancer and it gave me a sense of satisfaction, knowing that they would see how my hard work had paid off.

When it was time to leave to join the show, I travelled down to London with my Mum on the coach to Victoria Station; we walked the short distance from the coach station to the train station where I was going to get the train from London Victoria to Paris, Gare Du Nord.

Mum suggested that we went for a nice breakfast in the Hotel there at Victoria train station ahead of me travelling on the train and that's what we did. Inside the Hotel it was lovely, a little bit of luxury away from all the hustle and bustle. Mum and I always loved to do these little luxurious treats whenever we could.

Mum was always so supportive in any ways that she could be. It wasn't easy for her, because at the time my younger brother was only around 7 years old and Dad was never very helpful.

When I look back he could have offered to drive me down to London, but he never did. I suppose he spent a lot of his working week travelling up and down motorways in his car so he didn't feel like it, but if it was one of my children heading overseas on a contract, I would jump at the chance to spend time together in the car chatting before I waved them off for several months.

After breakfast I headed off to find my platform to catch the train to Paris, there I found Annette on the platform; we recognized each other from the audition at Pineapple studios. Annette was a pretty dark haired girl with big saucer brown eyes. She was the second youngest in the show after me and remarkably we shared the same birthday, September 25th. We also ended up sharing a room together in our accommodation. She was always a very quiet girl and very private.

I said my tearful farewell to dear Mum and she headed on down to see Surrey to see her Mum Gertrude or 'Nanny Foot' as we called her, who was now in a care home.

It was a sad situation for Mum that her Mum was in a nursing home, no one wants that for their loved ones, but the care required often demands it. Living in Stoke-on-Trent as Mum did, she tried to travel down to see her Mum as often as she could, every few weeks on the train or coach, since she did not drive.

I don't remember a lot about the train journey, I talked to Annette a little and then dosed off. Once we arrived in Paris and disembarked from the train we met the other new dancers from England who had also been on the train somewhere but in different coaches. Remember at that time, there were not mobile phones to message one another or connect.

Lee was a tall, striking, blonde girl from Essex, she was quite nurturing and motherly and loved to call everyone babe, she always seemed to be sucking the life out of a cigarette. Helen was from the Isle of Man with stunning long legs and the face of a model with chiseled cheekbones. The other Helen who we decided to call Liz (because it was too confusing having two Helens and Elizabeth was her middle name) was a natural beauty, she had the most amazing warm smile that literally lit up the room, a sunny personality and a huge sense of humor, she was always laughing and her and I hit it off immediately.

We headed to the Hotel where the management had organized for us to stay for the rehearsal period and I shared a room with Annette. On the first night we went to the restaurant in the hotel for dinner and I remember seeing snails for the first time, they looked revolting. I did try them and with a bit of garlic butter they are quite tasty but the texture I still find a bit off-putting and rubbery like.

The next morning we woke up and got ourselves ready to go and start rehearsals. I felt nervous as usual for the first day of rehearsals, it was not about my dancing ability, but I had been back at home not dancing much and had gained a few pounds again, so I was worried that I would look too heavy currently for a dancer. I was definitely one of the curviest dancers at the start of the contract, costume fittings started almost immediately on the first day and the wardrobe mistress, an old French lady called Gaby, was tutting and saying in French to slim down a bit. My French was very good having studied it at school and it was my favourite subject. Fortunately, as soon as the intense rehearsal period starts, you start to lose weight quickly dancing all day long.

There were around 20 dancers in the show; I was the youngest member of the show, 18 years old.

Other than the five of us who had come from UK, the others were already living in Paris, some had worked at La Nouvelle Eve before and so were returning for the new season and some had transferred from other shows. One of the first dancers that I recall chatting to was Jeanette, who we nicknamed Nettie, she was a tall, beautiful, sassy Australian dancer who had already worked in most of the shows such as the Moulin Rouge and the Lido. She seemed very worldly and was very friendly. I remember her saying that she couldn't believe how many different dialects and accents there were from the British girls and how hard it was to understand us at times. Not something we notice too much ourselves, but it is so true.

We warmed up in the auditorium, the showroom was an intimate theatre and very unique, obviously in the daytime the showrooms look far shabbier, but by nighttime it feels completely different. Our stage that we danced upon was actually thick tempered glass that lit up changing colours throughout the show and to this day it remains the same, it really is like no other show room that I have ever seen anywhere in the world, it is truly beautiful. Inside, the decor is sumptuous, giving this Parisian showroom a unique style.

Moulin Rouge

Stephanie was the tall and stunning Principal dancer at La Nouvelle Eve. To be a principal dancer, you needed to obviously be an outstanding dancer and perform topless. You should also be beautiful and very tall; the principals were amongst the tallest in order to also stand out. Stephanie was all of those things. During rehearsals, Stephanie suggested and organized for us to all go to see the Moulin Rouge show where she had previously worked. Obviously once our show opened we would not have the opportunity since we would be performing ourselves every night.

Most people have heard about the Moulin Rouge and *"Les Doriss girls"* it has the reputation of being the most famous cabaret in the world.

There have been several movies made about it and it has always had extravagant, wonderful stage settings, beautiful girls gracing the stage in magnificent costumes adorned with feathers, rhinestones sequins and the very famous French cancan, immortalized by the painter Toulouse-Lautrec. It is based in the Pigalle area of Paris, very close to La Nouvelle Eve.

I sat in anticipation waiting for this world famous cabaret to begin. As the curtain opened there was a line up of beautiful showgirls all with naked breasts. There were always dressed and topless dancers in the big famous Parisian shows, topless dancers were sometimes called 'nudes.' This was the first time that I had seen topless showgirls but I immediately thought how elegant and beautiful it all looked.

Unless you have seen a Parisian revue its hard to imagine how beautiful and artistically the topless showgirls are presented. The stunning feathers and huge jewels draped around the high kicking showgirls almost make you forget that they have artfully naked breasts as they glide around the stage.

Even so, I did not want to do this myself and was very definite in my mind that I would always be a dressed dancer.

I was horrified a few days later in rehearsals when I learned that EVERYONE had to be topless for the final walk down in the grand finale feather routine at La Nouvelle Eve. "But I was contracted as a dressed dancer," I cried to Annette. "Don't worry, its only one routine and just a short walk around the stage right at the very end of the show," Annette tried to reassured me.

After a while you honestly do just get used to it and don't really notice; the only time I felt embarrassed was when my Mum came to see the show with Aunty Jean and Elaine, her two best friends.

I never did topless again after La Nouvelle Eve, even though I was offered to. I didn't feel confident enough.

Our dressing room was a few flights of stairs up in the building, the dancers are always the furthest away from the stage, so as soon as we came off stage from one dance routine, we had to run frantically up the stairs, undressing as we ran and then quickly change into our next costume and run down the stairs again in record time ready for our next routine. There was no way that you could *not* lose weight, doing this for two shows every night. Particularly in this show, we performed the most incredible, energetic French cancan.

This famous fast and furious dance originally performed by local Parisian ladies. The cancan is a swirling multicoloured mix of skirts and petticoats, frilly pants, garters and stockings. All shown off by the dancers performing high kicks, cartwheels, hopping around on one leg, with the other leg raised and held high against our shoulders like a rifle, then jumping high into the air and landing violently down on the stage in the splits, accompanied with squeals of excitement and whooping.

It is the most energetic routine in the show.

Every rehearsal and indeed every show I both dreaded it and loved it in equal measures. Luis Diaz who was the choreographer at the time, would shout at the top of his voice in French *"Vas-y! Vas-y!"* Which roughly translates as *"Go on! Go on!"* Gesturing for us to kick our legs faster and faster, higher and higher.

I was always extremely flexible and enjoyed shouldering my leg up to my ear and hopping around, cartwheeling and jumping into the splits, for the slightly less flexible dancers I think it was quite a painful dance and we had to be super warmed up in order to perform it 100% and not to endure injuries, that said, there were always some pulled hamstrings here and there.

This explosive dance would get everyone in the audience excited from all over the world and often gained a standing ovation.

By the time opening night came around, I had lost weight and felt good, but obviously I wanted to lose some more weight, dancers always do!

Liz and I were backstage doing our final warm up and we found a safe place where we could peak out from behind the curtain and see the audience looking elegant dressed up clinking their glasses in anticipation of the show. They were sitting around the small rectangular tables with crisp white tablecloths and softly lit tiny lamps. The first show of the night included dinner and the second show, which started at around 11 p.m., was the champagne show with drinks only.

We all took our places on stage behind the curtain, there were lots of shouts of *"merde"* which is the traditional French way to say 'good luck' for shows, a bit like the Brits saying "break a leg." We heard the soon to become familiar announcement in several languages informing the audience that it was forbidden to take photos or videos of the performers and the show. Then suddenly the backstage lights dimmed, the curtain whooshed open and a million bright lights lit up the stage and us in our sparkling costumes, we all burst into singing the opening song in French

"*Strass et paillettes, magnifique toilette, fantasies parisiennes ...*" which roughly translates as, "*rhinestones, sequins, magnificent costumes, Parisian Fantasies ...*"

I always loved the excitement of curtain up, the exhilaration of performing and wowing audiences is like nothing else I have ever experienced. I truly loved my life as a dancer and felt so lucky to be getting paid to do something that I loved so much, whilst seeing the world.

It was very expensive to rent an apartment in Paris, so the management advised that it would be a good idea for the five of us dancers that had all traveled over together from England to share. Adrien one of our bosses helped us to find a couple of possible apartments during our rehearsal period and we chose one, which had two bedrooms and a lounge that could be used as a bedroom. We agreed to take the apartment and moved in swiftly. The apartment was on the 5th floor and we had to walk up a wooden spiral staircase to reach it. It was extremely tiring walking up 5 flights of stairs, even for us fit dancers, I always used to stop half way up for a little breather, but I kept thinking this is also great to keep us fit and lose more weight. I actually thought no wonder its vacant, not many people would want to walk up quite so many stairs. Inside it was very spacious and you could see that it had once been very elegantly decorated; now it was dated but still a beautiful property.

I would love to go back and redecorate that apartment; it could be stunning if it wasn't rented out and with a little money spent on it and I love doing interiors. The kitchen and dining room had windows that looked out over a courtyard area, which was overlooked by windows from other surrounding apartments. I rarely spotted anyone through the windows, sometimes though; we heard the most magnificent opera singing. A deep strong Opera voice echoed around the courtyard and rose up towards our windows and apartment. We never found out who he was, but the voice was outstanding.

At the apartment, Annette and I shared the twin room, Helen took the lounge as her bedroom with the sofa bed and Lee and Liz who had known each other and worked together before on another contract, took the other bedroom that had a double bed. They were happy to share the double bed; dancers were like that we were always sharing beds with each other, like a big gang of sisters.

The apartment was expensive and we had to pay a large deposit, which we could not afford, so the management paid this and we paid them back monthly out of our salary.

Our new apartment was in the 10th Arrondissement of Paris, it was very much a local's area and there weren't any tourist attractions in this area. It had a large Arabic influence; the majority of the shops had Arabic writing in the windows and Arabic owners. There were fantastic fresh fruit and vegetable markets in Rue du Faubourg Saint-Denis, the next street to ours and we would go there most days to buy food from the market and our local supermarket, Monoprix. Liz always used to say that it reminded her of being back in Damascus, the capital of Syria, where she had recently done a contract. It's hard to imagine nowadays that there were fine hotels and lavish cabaret shows in Syria. In recent years we only ever hear about tragedy and war in Syria.

The market stall owners were friendly and kind to us, they always used to throw us extra grapefruits or a few apples in with our shopping free of charge.

Rue Des Paradis was also quite near to Gare Du Nord train Station. I walked up there and remembered Erin and me sitting cold at the station on our way home from the ridiculous Italian dancing job. I felt so happy and relieved that things had turned out well and I was now working for a good reputable show in Paris.

Our bosses, were Adrien and Bernard Pierini, two good looking brothers. Several of the dancers had warned us that they were known to be 'playboys' even though they were both in long term relationships with their girlfriends who were both in the show.

Soon after the show had opened and we had started the season, a very small group of us were invited back to one of the male dancers home for drinks after the show. One of the bosses was giving me a lot of attention, he was actually good fun and easy to get along with. "Let me show you the view through here," he said, beckoning me away from the group into another room, he showed me indeed a great view and then tried to kiss me! "Stop it," I said, "we can't do that!" He laughed and said, "why not?" pressing his lips down on mine, but I pulled away, pointing out that he had a girlfriend and it would be wrong.

I didn't want to lose my job, I felt that I needed to try and get out of this politely somehow, without denting his ego. "I have a boyfriend who is coming over to see me soon." I lied.

I managed to detangle myself somehow and Liz and I headed home in a taxi.

I told Liz on the way home and she was shocked too.

I felt nervous going into work the next day, I was worried about repercussions, since I had rejected one of my bosses advances, but I needn't have worried.

He was completely normal and paid me no extra attention what-soever and did not seem embarrassed in any way. I just put it down to drunken behaviour.

Then a week or two later, I found out that one of the other dancers was now secretly having a relationship with him!

A couple of weeks into the show opening, we heard that a few danc-ers from the Paradis Latin show were in the audience watching our show. There's nothing like knowing other dancers are in the audience to make everyone perform that extra mile. In Paris most of the shows did not close for a single night, but most of the shows gave their artists a night off on a rota basis, there would be what we called 'swing' dancers who learned multiple positions in the show so that they could fill in if people were off. At La Nouvelle Eve, we had no swing and zero nights off.

Even if we felt ill, we somehow had to put a smile on our faces and get through the show, there was no such thing as calling in sick. Fortunately, once we are on stage we forget about any pain.

Afterwards a few of the dancers who knew them said they had arranged for us all to go and meet up straight after the show for drinks to Le Palmier Café. We walked the very short distance to Le Palmier that was just between La Nouvelle Eve and Moulin Rouge and where lots of show people gathered for after show drinks. One of them was a British male dancer who everyone called Lamb. He was very confident but also friendly and interesting to talk to. As newbie dancers in Paris, we loved learning about the other shows. He immediately took a shine to my beautiful friend Liz. They met up again and a few days later he came over to our apartment to see her. While we were in the kitchen he said to me, "You are an amazing talented dancer, you are one of the very best dancers on the stage in that show!" I was so proud, everyone knew that the dancers from Paradis Latin were incredible and he was praising me! Then he continued *"but its no good filling up your cupboard with mars bars, you need to be thinner."*

My bubble was completely burst and I felt crushed. I instantly forgot about the praise for my dancing and could only focus on the fact that he had said I should lose more weight. I locked myself in the bathroom and cried.

Plus, I genuinely was not eating any chocolate bars; my food mostly consisted of grapefruits, marmite on toast for breakfast, an omelette or salad before the show and a yoghurt, with an apple or other fruit.

I had also already joined a nearby gym and every day I would go and exercise after breakfast and do various dance classes too after my gym workout before our 2 shows a night.

However, you can never be too thin when you are a dancer.

Interestingly, this year, my husband Tom and I decided to go and stay at one of the very best health clinics in the world, Clinique La Prairie in Switzerland. Part of the programme that we signed up for was genetic investigations. I discovered that I have the highest genetic predisposition to be overweight and obese! This was SO interesting to discover and it made a lot of sense to me. It doesn't mean that you have to be overweight or obese, but it means that genetically it is so much harder *not* to be. After all these years I finally felt that I had verification, that's why I could eat and drink the same as other dancers, or indeed less, but still struggle with my weight.

Extreme Diet

In Paris, I decided I would go on an *extreme* diet I had recently read about, the orange fast diet, where you ate nothing except oranges for 5 days. "Right," I thought, "that's easy enough to stick to." So the next morning I went to the market with Liz and bought LOTS of oranges, I cant quite remember how many but a few kilos worth, our market stall holders were surprised and he checked with me a couple of times to make sure I hadn't said the wrong amount. *"Oui oui,"* I assured him with a smile. The oranges were heavy to carry home, especially up our 5 flights of spiral stairs. I embarked on my orange fast and started losing more weight, around day 3 I did feel a little fed up of only eating oranges but I could see that my costumes were getting looser and that gave me the greatest incentive to continue. Looking back, I'm amazed that I managed to perform two highly energetic shows a night having only eaten oranges. My day 5 fell on a Friday. I was ecstatic to have finished my orange fast and it was a *Soiree* night at La Nouvelle Eve after the show and we decided that tonight we would attend.

Each month on some of the Fridays after our shows had finished, La Nouvelle Eve would hold *soirees,* which basically meant that La Nouvelle Eve transformed into a sort of super elegant nightclub. I couldn't believe how dressed up the people were, almost costume like in fabulous outfits. Everyone bought drinks and then our stage was used as the dance floor.

Liz and I weren't in the habit of drinking too much alcohol, so it was a real *"let your hair down"* kind of night for us. I'm sure even without doing the orange fast that I would have been worse for wear drinking lots of alcohol, but because I had only eaten oranges for the previous five days, I got absolutely obliterated drunk!

I can't remember everything, but I do remember dancing lots on the stage and having so much fun. Then I felt ill, everything was spinning around and I felt sick, I couldn't see Liz anywhere, so I decided I would head up to the safety of our dressing room and have a little lie down. The next thing I recall is Liz finding me lying on the floor of our dressing room and trying to wake me up to go home, she had enlisted the help of Umberto the stage manager and a couple of other stagehands, thank goodness. It's all blurry but I recall they somehow managed to get me home in a car. The worst bit of course was since I was legless; quite literally, they had to carry me up the 5 flights of spiral staircases! Poor them and thank goodness I was now quite skinny and didn't weigh too much, bless them.

I think I've never been more appreciative. Or embarrassed. The following day of course I had to do the show, I found Umberto backstage to thank him and apologize. He just laughed it off. He was a genuinely kind person.

Each night As soon as our second show finished, everyone very quickly removed their eyelashes, fishnet tights were hung up and there was a mad rush for the sinks and showers.

As we exited the side door of La Nouvelle Eve, we were barely recognizable without the glamorous show make up, eyelashes and hair scraped off our faces in a ponytail, dressed in tracksuits. Unless we were heading out for the night obviously.

Liz and I used to walk home together after the show, the walk took us around 20 minutes we rarely ever took a taxi, we were always conscious of saving money and to be honest we enjoyed winding down and chatting after two shows, its hard to go straight to sleep as soon as you finish work and especially 2 adrenalin filled magnificent shows. Also, since we were seated at opposite ends of the large dressing room far away from one another, we enjoyed exchanging gossip about who had said what to whom.

One of the questions that I have been asked many times is about cattiness and rivalry working with so many girls in such a competitive industry, but I can honestly say that was hardly ever my experience thankfully in my dancing career.

Sometimes it felt a little scary walking through the Parisian streets at around 1.00 a.m. But Liz and I always walked home together and we always had our keys in our hands, as instructed by Nettie, in case anyone attacked us, "poke them straight in the eyes with the keys," she advised, something I've always remembered. I also bought and carried a small atomizer of mace spray, which is a type of pepper spray that can be used by spraying it in the face of an attacker, which temporarily blinds them so that you can run away, thankfully I never had to use either.

Back at the apartment, Liz and I would sometimes share a bottle of cheap French wine and I would cook omelettes with strong stinky French cheeses inside and we would chat about the shows and the audiences that night.

If it were someone's birthday then we would happily go and celebrate at a chosen restaurant. La Cloche d'or was my absolute favourite restaurant, which was virtually next door to La Nouvelle Eve situated in Rue Mansart.

The Cloche D'Or, which means *the golden bell,* was a fantastic little restaurant and is still there now, I would love to return one day. The food always tasted outstanding with deep-fried Camembert being a firm favourite entrée, although I usually ate melon to start since I was now super conscious about my very svelte figure. The kitchen here remained open until really late, so it was perfect for late night show people and was always busy with dancers from several Parisian shows. We celebrated a lot of cast members' birthdays here and I celebrated my own 19th birthday here on September 25th which I shared with Annette my roommate who had the same birthday.

Sometimes during the day, we would go for a picnic next to the river Seine; Liz introduced me to *Boursin,* a rich garlicky cheese that I still love, thank you Liz. We would take with us a French stick, a box of Boursin and sometimes a bottle of wine. It was so simple but so good, and so French. Sitting by the river Seine in the warm sunshine, it never tasted better.

I was very excited that my Mum was coming to see me along with my Godmother, Aunty Jean and her other best friend Elaine. I had found a small guesthouse in our actual street Rue De Paradis. They had a triple room on the top floor that had three beds in it and so I booked this room for them for the weekend.

None of my family had seen me in the first professional shows in Spain that I had danced in. So I was super excited for Mum to be seeing me now in a Professional show in Paris. Mum had always encouraged, supported and helped me with every single audition since I was a small child so it must have been quite something for her to be seeing the fruits of her labour too and her daughter dancing up on stage in a world class Parisian show.

My big brother Adey also came over to see the show and me. It was great having them to visit, because it gave me a chance do lots of touristy things in the daytime, like visiting Notre Dame and the Eifel Tower amongst other sites.

As dancers, we all lead very different lives to most other people, when they were winding down for bed; we were heading up to the Pigalle area where La Nouvelle Eve was, to start ShowTime.

Liz was honestly my lifeline in Paris, such a sweet, kind friend. At 18 we think we are grown up and mature, but we are not really. Nettie was an angel too and like a big sister to Liz and myself. Sometimes we would go over to Nettie's home that she shared with her French husband who was a musician and their absolutely gorgeous dog called Sydney. It was a touch of normality and felt 'family like' spending time at Nettie's home and she would cook something for us.

The end of the season was approaching so it was time to think about our next dancing contracts.

Nettie suggested that I wrote to Miss Doris at the Moulin Rouge to see if she was auditioning, which I did.

Audition with the Legendary Miss Doris at Moulin Rouge

Doris Haug or *Miss Doris* as she was known, is a very iconic and famous character in the history of the Moulin Rouge. She became known worldwide as the maitresse de ballet/ballet mistress at the Moulin Rouge, creating and choreographing *Les Doriss girls* (the spelling is correct; she is Miss Doris with only one 's' but as her dancers; we were called *Les Doriss girls,* with two s's on the end).

Born in Germany in 1927, Doris dreamed of one thing: dancing. Doris came to Paris aged 25 and passed her audition and fulfilled her dream of becoming a dancer at the famous Moulin Rouge. Rising through the ranks, she then moved on and formed her own dance troupe at the nearby La Nouvelle Eve and *Les Doriss girls* were born, with Doris at the helm as the ballet mistress.

In 1957 the Moulin Rouge recognized that she was the choreographer and Ballet Mistress required to regain prestige at the Moulin Rouge and she was head hunted and recruited by them. By 1961 she was co-creating and directing unforgettable show productions with her know-how, and she continued until 1997 when she retired aged 70.

So towards the end of our contract at La Nouvelle Eve, I sent a letter to Miss Doris, explaining that I was currently working as a dancer at La Nouvelle Eve and since our season was soon to be finishing, that I would like to audition to work for her.

Soon after I received an invitation to go and audition with her. I was both excited and nervous.

I made my way to the Moulin Rouge and was shown backstage through a labyrinth of dressing rooms where I was allowed to change. It was early in the day so there was hardly anyone there, just a few wardrobe mistresses repairing costumes.

The dressing rooms looked much like ours, with walls full of feather backpacks and headdresses and rail after rail of costumes.

It was an absolute amazing feeling, just being backstage at this world famous cabaret, as I changed I thought about all of the hundreds of dancers who would have done the same over the years since it first opened in 1889. If these walls could talk and tell stories, what secrets they must hold!

There were three of us auditioning, so after changing into dance clothes, we were taken on to the stage where we were told to warm up. I couldn't believe I was here on stage at The Moulin Rouge.

After a few minutes Miss Doris appeared in the auditorium and asked us to come down into the reception area of the Moulin Rouge, where she would audition us.

Miss Doris had a reputation for being abrupt, she was very direct which was fine if she liked you and was pleased with your performance, but if she thought you were not up to scratch, she would tell you directly.

Doris choreographed and put us through our paces, scrutinizing and observing our high kicks. I picked up the choreography easily thankfully. I walked elegantly like a showgirl should and danced confidently and I could see when she was watching me, that she seemed happy with my performance. At the end of the audition, she finished off making us all do cartwheels around the reception area and then she offered me a job and contract straight away! I was bursting with excitement.

I asked her if she had any positions in her show in Monaco available, Nettie had worked there and said, "Try to go to the Folie Russe show that they own also in Monaco. It's so much fun and you do only one show a night, a night off every week and its more money than the Moulin." Miss Doris said that she would find out and then let me know whether or not she needed me for Paris at the Moulin or Monte Carlo, for the Folies Russe show. I was on cloud nine.

To the boy dancer who had auditioned she said in her slightly stern Germanic accent, "You are not a dancer. If I want to be a painter I need to know how to paint; if you want to be a dancer you need to know how to dance and you don't." Brutal honesty.

In recent years when I have watched talent shows on TV and see the panel of judges such as Simon Cowell, I think he is like a pussycat compared to Miss Doris!

Meanwhile, Liz went to audition at the Crazy Horse, where the most beautiful girls in the world are recruited and she was offered a place immediately and had a hugely successful career there for several years.

The Crazy Horse show is a very prestigious show situated on the Avenue George V. In Paris. It has attracted, famous celebrities and tourists from all over the world since it opened and continues to do so. The showroom is quite small and intimate for a Paris showroom. It has a small stage and the choreography was very sensual and daring in an erotic way, but never trashy or tacky. The dancers were generally nude, with stunning accessories and the creative lighting is done in such a way that that it 'dresses' the girls. Everyone knew that the Crazy Horse girls were treated like royalty, there were cars and drivers to take the dancers safely home and between the shows, dinner was provided from the restaurant next door and most of all, they were paid far more than any other show anywhere.

The stunning girls who dance in the show were all hand picked by the owner Mr. Alain Bernardin. He gave all of the girls a stage name, Liz told me that he had given her a couple to choose from, but she told him cheekily that she didn't really like them and suggested instead that she could be called *Betty Buttocks,* which is a nickname that I had made up for Liz once we heard the exciting news that she had been selected to be a Crazy Horse girl. Unbelievably Mr. Bernardin agreed. So I actually baptized a Crazy Horse girl, "Betty Buttocks".

I was on my way to sign my contract with Miss Doris who lived in Montmartre. I walked past the Moulin Rouge, noticing how dirty everything around me in Pigalle looked during the daytime without the charm of the nighttime neon lights. There were several sex shops and strip clubs dotted around between the bars and cafes.

I started walking up a steep road with lots of old steps towards the Montmartre area nearby where she lived. Doris greeted me at the door and showed me into her apartment, she was hobbling a little because at the time she had a cast on one foot, I asked her what she had done and she said that she had tripped down the stairs that lead to her lower level basement area. I sat down in a lounge area, noticing beautiful black and white photos of her adorning the walls, from her own days as a dancer. How wonderful it must feel, I thought, to have started out as a dancer and now be the *maitresse de ballet* at the Moulin Rouge and the other shows. There was a wooden desk, piled high with lots of dancer's CVs on; I wanted to pinch myself again. I remember to the right of me, there was a hatch and some steps that went down to a basement area, which must have been where she fell, and I could hear her dog. We had a small chat, and she gave me some helpful information about Monte Carlo and the Folie Russe show before she produced my contract which I then signed feeling ecstatic. She gave me the contacts of the head dancer in Monaco, J.C. and told me that I was to contact her. She also gave me a business card with her own contact details on for her Monaco residence and said that she would be in Monaco soon and see me again at rehearsals. I thanked her and said Goodbye.

The last few weeks flew by, I was put in touch with a Dutch dancer called Akke from Monaco who was leaving the show to come and dance in Paris, so I arranged with her that I would take over her studio apartment. The last night of the show was full of the usual fun and frolics, laughs and tears, as we all packed up our dressing tables and make up boxes and said our farewells.

We ended the season on a high, Liz and I both had our wonderful contracts to go to and our dear friend Nettie shared the lovely and exciting news that she was pregnant with her first baby.

Paris had been an amazing experience for me. I had learned so much.

I had not had any exciting romantic encounters whatsoever in this city that ironically everyone associates with romance. We had not done much socialising or partying, but I had managed to save a fair amount of money and was leaving; stick thin, which made me extremely happy of course.

Liz and I packed up our belongings and spent our last night at dear Nettie's house. We left Paris together and headed back to the UK on a hovercraft.

I spent around two weeks back in Stoke-on-Trent with my family and sadly I was sick during this period and was unable to go and see my dearest Liz who had invited me to celebrate her 21st birthday with her in Gloucestershire. Miraculously Dad had even offered to give me a lift to go and see Liz which is probably why I remember this so clearly since it was such a rarity for him to offer lifts!

The night before I left for Monaco, Dad took us all out for a nice family dinner and we all scrubbed up smartly and went to the Borough Arms Hotel in Newcastle-under-Lyme, the photo is in the book here and on the wall is an oil painting that moved around with us from home to home and was always above the fireplace.

Recently, Mum downsized her home and sold the painting to a dealer in Jersey since she had no place for it. When I found this out, I secretly bought it back and hung it on the bedroom wall here in the guest room of our Dubai home. Imagine her surprise when she came to visit, and it was now here.

On my way down to Monaco, I was lucky enough to be able to catch up and stay for a night in Paris with Nettie. It was great to see her and obviously since she had worked at the Folie Russe show that I was now joining, she gave me all the information that she could possibly think of that would be helpful.

I also had chance to catch up with my dear friend Liz who was already back in Paris and had started rehearsals at The Crazy Horse. Liz asked if I could be allowed to watch rehearsals, since I had to leave that evening on my way to join the Folie Russe show. Mr. Bernardin the boss usually never allowed anyone to watch she told me, he was very strict about this and so I was very privileged to be allowed to watch. During the rehearsals, I was introduced to Mr. Bernardin; he was very friendly and asked me with a cheeky smile, did I want to audition for the show?

Recently, Tom and I stayed at the Four Seasons George V Hotel; just opposite The Crazy Horse show which is still there, and I remembered fondly watching "Betty" perform and meeting Mr. Bernardin.

CHAPTER FIVE

Monte Carlo – Monaco

MY ADDRESS

17 Avenue de L'Annonciade, apt 16 number 8, 98000, Monaco

was on my way to the tiny principality of Monaco; the worlds second smallest country after the Vatican and ruled by Prince Rainier who had been married to the late Princess Grace.

When I arrived there, locals still talked about how wonderful the Princess was and they were still sad that she had died in a car accident with her daughter Princess Stephanie, alongside her in the car, who survived the accident.

For the rehearsal period, I stayed in a small Hotel in Beausoleil called Hotel Diana, along with Jen a very tall, pretty dancer from USA and a classically trained Dutch dancer called Monique.

Beausoleil is actually in France, but when you cross over the road you are then in the principality of Monaco. It's so strange, there are no borders, but once you have crossed over the road into Monaco there are different post boxes and postage stamps, because you are in fact in a different country.

I walked the short distance from the accommodation in Beausoleil to the Loews Hotel in Monaco to start rehearsals, I remember thinking how beautiful it was everywhere, very clean and manicured with lots of beautiful palm trees around, it was so different from Paris and the southern French coast weather was still sunny and warm too for October.

I vividly remember on that first morning walking to rehearsals, thinking again how lucky I was to be living this amazing life as a dancer.

Loews Hotel – 12 Avenue des Spelugues, 98000, Monaco

The Loews hotel in Monte Carlo was a very famous hotel, It had spectacular views of the Mediterranean sea and its own in-house casino, several restaurants and cocktail bars and of course our elegant show room where the *Folie Russe* show was Performed.

Running underneath the Hotel is a long tunnel, known then as the Loews tunnel. The tunnel is the most famous feature on the legendary Monaco Grand Prix formula 1 race circuit. The cars blast through it full throttle and it is a very well-known Hotel worldwide due to this.

As I'm writing the book, the former Loews Hotel, is now called the Fairmont Monte Carlo.

Recently my husband Tom and I stayed there in a suite. It was surreal actually being a guest. I had never seen any of the bedrooms in the hotel. I walked down to where our show room used to be and it was now a conference area. How sad I thought.

The once elegant piano bar in the lobby area has now been turned into a sports type bar with large TV screens showing sporting events.

I thought back to how elegant it used to be with the piano in there and the jazz singer Kenny Coleman crooning Frank Sinatra classics, whilst everyone was sipping Kir Royals and White Russian cocktails.

The Folie Russe show and stage area was much smaller than the Moulin Rouge, but we had the same type of specialty acts who would rotate frequently, imagine my surprise when I discovered that one of the new acts joining the show was El Gran Picaso, the amazing ping pong juggler from my first show in Spain. I was so happy to see him again and I think he was happy also to have a familiar face there.

The rehearsal period was intense for myself, Jen and Monique. We would rehearse during the day and then come to watch the show at night. As a dancer it's very difficult to sit and watch a live show and simply enjoy it, we notice everything, all the small details that other audience members would not notice. We analyze the choreography and costumes, how quick the changes are, which performers are outstanding on stage, but mostly we appreciate and respect the hard work.

Rehearsals started well for me. J.C. our dance captain was a no nonsense British girl who put us through our paces and then showed us around the Loews Hotel, introducing us to various staff members as we went along. A few other dancers wandered in occasionally during rehearsals, checking us out, probably silently giving us marks out of ten, seeing how we compared appearance wise. This was completely normal, in a world where we were completely judged by our looks and bodies, initially, then dance ability.

A few days in, J.C. called a company rehearsal for the whole cast of dancers and Miss Doris herself was in town and called in to watch some of the rehearsals. Everyone suddenly found an extra surge of energy from somewhere and performed to a higher standard when Miss Doris was watching and no one dared put a foot wrong.

I loved the new choreography, except one routine where we had to dance on top of small bentwood chairs, trying not to fall off obviously in our heels and then step down on to the stage and lean forward with our legs astride and pull the chair through our legs and flip it into the air balancing it high on our wrists. Hard to explain in words but believe me every night I could feel my heart pounding when this part of the routine approached. The show was a much slower pace than Paris, there was no high energy cancan and our dressing room was a few paces away from the stage, which was great, but not as great for burning calories. Everything was far more leisurely in comparison.

As well as rehearsals in the daytime, we had various medicals and paperwork that we needed to complete in order to be allowed to work in Monaco, so we were busy running around during the daytime organising this too. I remember walking back up the hill after one of these medicals and stopping at a zebra crossing between Hotel de Paris and the Casino de Monte Carlo. Boris Becker the famous tennis player pulled up in a new BMW and stopped at the zebra crossing for me. How funny I thought, he had recently moved to Monaco as a resident too.

I had already arranged to rent my small studio in Monaco with Akke who was leaving to go and join the Crazy Horse show in Paris. What a small dancers world it was, she was on her way up to Paris and about to meet and dance together with my dear friend Liz.

I loved my studio apartment in L'Annonciade and the luxury of living by myself after the sharing in Paris. At the time it was the tallest building in Monaco, although I'm sure that by now it has probably been superseded.

In my first week at the show in Monaco; I set off for the short 10-minute walk to work. I left my Studio apartment at L'Annonciade and walked along Boulevard Des Moulin's, when suddenly a brand new black Porsche pulled up alongside me right by Place Des Moulin's and the window lowered, How funny I thought they are going to ask me for directions and I've only been here a week and don't even know my own way around except how to get to the Loews Hotel. My French was not bad having studied at school and just danced for a season In Paris. I was surprised when the handsome young man, probably about 25, spoke to me in perfect English.

"Hello, I was wondering if I could give you a lift to work, I'm Christophe and I knew Akke, the dancer who you replaced and who lived in your apartment before you. I live in that same apartment block also." Blimey, I thought, he hasn't wasted much time.

I was stunned, I felt flattered but a little nervous, but if he knew Akke I decided he must be OK. I accepted and jumped into his car, my heart was pounding a bit with a mixture of excitement and nerves. He drove me the short distance to the Hotel chatting and when we arrived at the Hotel he said. "My father is having a private birthday ball tonight at The Monte Carlo Casino, I was wondering if you would like to come and be my guest after the show has finished?"

"Thank you for the invitation," I replied, "I'd love to but I'm not really dressed appropriately, look at what I'm wearing, I think I'm a little under-dressed." I was wearing black trousers, a crisp white shirt and a black cash-mere blazer. Smart enough to wander through the hotel, but I wouldn't have dreamt of turning up in something like that to a birthday dinner party in Stoke-on-Trent, let alone Monte Carlo.

"That doesn't matter at all," he said, "You are my guest and it's my father's party so just ask for me on the door and I'll come and meet you, it will be fine," he said reassuringly.

The show finished and I walked nervously next door from the Loews Hotel up a few steps to the Monte Carlo casino. The lady on the reception looked me up and down, unsurprisingly.

"I'm a guest of Christophe—" I started to say and before she could even say anything, Christophe appeared around the corner and kissed me on both cheeks French style and took my hand and led me into the birth-day party.

I had never seen so many beautiful looking people in one room. Everyone was dressed in beautiful gowns of course—I mean we are talking serious Monaco glamour and royalty and of course all dripping with jew-els. Lots of eyes fell upon me as Christophe led me to his father's top table, which was in the middle of the room, I felt ridiculous dressed in my casual clothing, but everyone just smiled and seemed very welcoming. I was Christophe's guest, so I was immediately accepted. Maybe they thought that I had just flown in from the airport I hoped.

Christophe introduced me to his father and I wished him a happy birthday. We sat down at the end of the top table and Christophe poured me a glass of vintage Champagne and went around the table giving me the rundown of who was who in Monaco: "That's Bjorn Borgs ex-wife Mariana, she owns a night club here called Noroc, I'll take you one night. That's

Roberto Rossellini, he's Isabella Rossellini's son. That's Prince Albert over there, my friend and his father Prince Rainier just left..." It was like a scene from a movie, full of elegantly dressed, beautiful people, sipping champagne. Surreal is an understatement really of how I was feeling.

Could this be really happening to me? I was a 19-year-old girl from Stoke-on-Trent and here I was, a few days into my Monaco job, mixing with Europe's royalty and glitterati, unbelievable!

The following day I told one of the other friendly British dancers, Nicki, about the night before. Nicki was a gorgeous blonde haired dancer from the UK with an electric smile. She had attended Ballet Rambert and was an excellent dancer and stood out on stage with her beautiful technique. Nicki had been there a lot longer in Monaco and warned me off Christophe. She told me that although he was charming and good looking and well connected, he was one of Prince Albert's best friends, he had only recently been involved in a drugs scandal.

I did have a few more dates with Christophe, but I decided that he was complicated and to steer clear of him. It was a little difficult sometimes since I did bump into him in the lift a few times.

There were other men in Monaco that I dated, but none of them are worth mentioning. Most of the men that I met were either playboys or had wives tucked away at home somewhere that they were cheating on. I was very young and naïve, and it was a steep learning curve.

There was one guy who I did feel I had a genuine connection with, but he told me that since he was from such an aristocratic family, that he would not ever be allowed to marry a dancer.

"So, he is just using me," I thought and did not see him again. I wanted a meaningful relationship.

A few weeks later, I heard he was now using another dancer from our show!

After our first pay day, Jen and I decided to treat ourselves to dinner at one of Monaco's best restaurants. We were seated at a nice table and noticed that the elderly but very glamourous lady, dripping in diamonds behind us had brought her poodle with her and the poodle was sat at the table on a chair eating some kind of meat from a plate. Only in Monaco! How hilarious and weird. The restaurant was buzzy, full of locals, there was a table with two men who we noticed were looking over at us and smiling, they got up to leave before us, as they did one of them came over and introduced himself as Franck, he handed me a business card which said on it, "Two dinners offered for you tomorrow evening for your beautiful eyes." Life was never dull in Monaco!

Another evening when we arrived in to work, Monique did not turn up for the show, it was getting later and later. We waited and waited and she never showed up, so there was a frantic re-choreographing.

Eventually J.C. the dance captain managed to contact Monique's family and it turned out that Monique did a "bunk" as we called it when someone absconded and she went back home to Holland. She just decided that she felt out of place in the Monaco show, she was a very classically trained ballet dancer and didn't feel as though she was ever truly going to fit in.

A stunning red-haired dancer called Julie became one of my other closest friends from the show. Julie had a gorgeous Welsh accent. There were several older dancers in this show I noted, some were late thirties and early forties even, which for dancers was classed as getting old. They had fallen in love with husbands and the glamour of living in Monaco on the French Riviera. They would usually stay for their 2 drinks at the piano bar after the show and then head home to their families, while the rest of us who were young and single would go out dancing somewhere.

Both Nicki and Julie's boyfriends worked in the casino at Loews as croupiers. The croupiers did not finish work until very late when the casino closed, long after the show had finished, so we often went out together with others from the show.

Each night after our show finished, we were allowed 2 free drinks in the piano bar and it was here that my dear friend Nicki introduced me to the wonders of Kir Royals and White Russian cocktails, Grand Marnier and Sambuca! In Monaco it was a strict tradition that the Sambuca needed to have coffee beans floating in the drink and it must be an *uneven* number otherwise it was considered unlucky. In a casino town these things definitely matter.

Our favourite place to go next was called The Living Room and was very close to the hotel, just a couple of minutes walk up the hairpin band that is so famous in the Monaco Grand Prix, Avenue Des Spelugues. The Living Room, was a very glamorous Private club for the wealthy residents of Monaco.

The owner of the living room at the time, was a down to earth Italian man called Miguel, unlike the other Monaco residents he did not drive around in a super car, but instead he pootled around on a little moped.

He made it very clear that *Les Doriss girls* from the Folie Russe show were always welcome every night and we could have as much free champagne as we wanted. He knew that we could always be relied upon to come out looking glamourous, dance and party. We would go up there most nights and drink champagne and dance on the small dance floor, the waiters would bring out delicious smoked salmon finger sandwiches for us to nibble on.

The living room had a friendly doorman who was called Willy and Scottish.

He was there for years and years, even long after I left Monaco, I remember hearing from other people that had been to The Living Room in Monaco that Willy was still there. In around 2012, sadly I heard from a family friend that Willy had died.

Prince Albert and European Royalty

Prince Albert of Monaco could often be seen in the *Living Room* and a couple of dancers that I know dated him. He often came to watch the Folie Russe show. I was seated in a group around a table with him a couple of times but never really spoke to him other than to smile and say hello, I was just happy and excited to be part of it and experiencing all of this. I couldn't wait to tell Mum the stories. One of the other regulars in

The Living Room was Renato Roberto Rossilini who was the son of the world-famous Italian film director, screenwriter and producer Roberto Rossilini and Swedish movie star Ingrid Bergman. He was always friendly and always flirty with the ladies.

The night Life in Monaco was the opposite of my experience in Paris. Here, alcohol flowed freely, we never had to pay for anything and drugs were plentiful should you require them, which I did not.

Other titled European royalty that happened to be in town along with local residents all went to The living Room and often at the weekend we would carry on afterwards to the legendary JIMMYZ night club, nearby on Avenue Princesse Grace, or jump in friends prestige cars and head to Whisky a Gogo in Juan Les Pins, all frequented by beautiful and attractive famous locals.

Sometimes we would drive over the border and go the beautiful Italian casino in San Remo which was only around 30 minutes drive in a fast car, to dine in exclusive restaurants. I remember early on one of the older girls who had lived there for a few years saying to me, "Always carry your passport with you in your handbag darling, you never know where you are going to get whisked off to."

Everyone parked their super cars directly outside, drank all evening and then jumped straight in to their Ferraris and Porsches and drove back home. I'm not sure whether there were any drink driving rules in place, but if there were no one seemed to care. The roads in Monaco are winding and challenging as we can see in the famous Monaco F1. There were two well known, handsome local brothers, Jean Claude and Jean Pierre who were regulars and who socialized in our circle of friends and sadly I heard that one of the brothers did tragically die in a car accident a few years later.

One night, Julie and I started to walk home we'd had drinks at the Loews and a couple at The Living Room. We passed one of our other favourite restaurants that we frequented regularly where we knew all of the waiters and staff. They had an outside area for dining and here there was always a large sweet trolley on wheels housing fabulous cakes and desserts. For some reason, probably the large amount of Kir Royals that we had drank; we decided that it would be hilarious to steal a whole chocolate cake. There was no one else outside, so we quickly took it and ran up the hill squealing with laughter imagining the face of whichever waiter found the entire cake missing. This was Monaco and no one stole things. I remember we had to sit on the floor we were laughing so much we could not walk or talk. We were devouring the chocolate cake sat on the pavement with our hands; it tasted so good and eventually when we were full, we put the rest in a bin and walked home. The next day we both felt very guilty of course and went and owned up immediately and apologized offering to pay. Luckily for us, the restaurant weren't bothered at all and found it very funny and wouldn't hear of taking any payment, instead inviting us in and offering us free drinks.

At the beginning of December, my big brother Adey came over to visit. It was the run up to Christmas, and I told Luigi One of the waiters from the *Living Room* who was chubby, smiley and friendly that my brother was over visiting. He said "Come with your brother after the show and have a cup of champagne and a piece of *pannetone*," Since it was near to Christmas they were serving traditional Italian Christmas cake pannetone with champagne as snacks for the guests. A new family tradition was born! Since then, to this very day, Adey and I always make it a tradition to toast each other with a cup of champagne and a piece of pannetone around Christmas time.

While Adey was over visiting me, there was great excitement at the show, because it was suddenly announced that we were to be given a couple of days off from the show due to essential maintenance work. Most of the dancers started whispering excitedly about going over to ski nearby at Limone Piemonte, which was only just over the Italian border, about an hours drive away by car.

We were strictly forbidden to ski, and it was written in our contracts.

Obviously, if we had accidents and broke any limbs then we would be out of the show for a long time. Obviously, being young and adventurous, we took no notice whatsoever.

One dancer even broke a rib but still continued to do the shows, drugged up with strong painkillers, too afraid to confess since she knew that she would have been fired.

Ade and I decided that we would go too. We took the train from Monaco to Italy, changing at Ventimiglia to Limone, it was an easy and enjoyable train journey going through tunnel after tunnel that had been burrowed through the spectacular mountains, it took around 3 and a half hours in total. As we disembarked in Limone we queued up to show our passports to the passport control immigration officers, while in the queue we saw a few other dancers in the queue and waved to one another excitedly.

It was such short notice, that most of the rooms were fully booked, we walked around the beautiful small snowy town and eventually found one room left, the lady on reception was calling us husband and wife and we laughed explaining that no we were actually brother and sister. We were just glad to have a bed and we managed to bunk up for a couple of nights and survive.

Limone Piemonte is one of the most beautiful places that I have *ever* been to. It is one of the oldest Alpine villages in Italy, with a small twelfth century church at its center. It was so traditional then, with the snow falling and the church bell chiming. There were only around 4 restaurants and a handful of small Hotels. I'm sure now it has probably expanded, but I really hope that it has kept its magic and not become too commercialized.

This was my first ever experience of a ski resort. Adey was already a very proficient skier, so he went off and enjoyed the snow while I pootled around and was happy most of the time sipping Coffee and sitting in a deckchair in my ski gear enjoying the rays of the sun reflecting off the crisp white snow.

One thing that I always remember was that you could buy these funny little silver foil cardboard collar things, for around a pound in UK currency but obviously then it was Italian Lira before the Euro, that you would put in front of your face to reflect the sun and intensify getting your face tanned. How ironic, now we are all always trying to keep our faces away from the suns rays to avoid wrinkling and sun damage, but back then it was *de rigeur* to have a tan, especially on your face.

This was my first Christmas away from home and it was fast approaching. There was a beautiful Christmas party organized for all of the hotel staff, which we were included in. They really were very generous to us all and we had a choice of gifts, either a small TV or a brand new Sony Walkman with headphones, which I chose.

Backstage in the dressing room we each chose a name from a hat for Secret Santa and wrapped and put our gifts under a little tree in the dressing room. The youngest person would then give out the gifts on Christmas Eve, which was me. I found out that Pat had chosen my name and she bought me a lovely bottle of O de Lancôme, a lovely fresh fragrance that to this day reminds me of Monaco whenever I smell it. I love how fragrances can instantly transport us back to a time or place.

On Christmas day itself, Gran Picasso had invited myself and Jen over to his accommodation and he cooked us food and we helped him with everything and all exchanged small gifts, but then of course we had a show to perform at night, which was great fun. This was my first Christmas spent apart from my family; I would subsequently spend many more away on dancing contracts.

The best Christmas present for me was that I received a letter from the Equity union telling me that following my contract at La Nouvelle Eve, along with my contract in Spain; I had now qualified for my full equity card. I was ecstatic to get my full Equity membership at such a young age.

Realistically this did not change my life one bit, but at the time it was deemed a big deal to have your Equity card and meant that you could apply for practically any job anywhere in the world. In reality, for me it meant that you paid an annual fee and if you ended up somewhere dodgy, like Turin, they were supposed to help you—but only if you were on an Equity approved contract. I paid my fees for quite a few years but then decided since I was not getting any benefit from it, to cease being a paid member.

Not long after Christmas, Nicki celebrated her 21st birthday and then decided soon after that she wanted to leave Monaco. I was truly sad to see her go but we promised to stay in touch. The next time I would actually see Nicki would be in Dubai many years later.

One evening in April, around Easter time Julie and I were sipping Champagne as usual after the show in the Living Room club and we got chatting to an Italian Doctor from San Remo. He said that he had seen the show and how much he had enjoyed it and that he recognized us. He seemed a polite man; he was in Monaco for work and asked if he could buy us some drinks. We enjoyed chatting to him; he wasn't trying to chat us up or sleazy in any way whatsoever. He then invited us to join him at the casino tables so we walked the very short distance over to the Monte Carlo casino. Luck was definitely on his side that night and he just kept winning and winning, he was playing and winning high stakes. He was so happy and said that Julie and I were definitely his lucky charms, insisting on giving both of us a large wad of money each and a chocolate Easter hamper, before driving off never to be seen again!

I was just so happy to be having fun and making the most of the nightlife in Monaco and the privileges that our *Doriss girls* status afforded us. I loved the glamourous social scene here and was more than making up for my lack of social life in Paris. It was a stark contrast to my contract in Paris where I had barely gone out other than an occasional birthday. Looking back I think I took these Monaco experiences in my stride the best I could considering my young age.

One of my most memorable performances in Monaco was at the annual Monaco International Circus Festival.

Started in 1974 by Prince Rainier III of Monaco, This event takes place every January in Monaco and circus performers from all over the world are invited to perform, with prestigious awards presented during a closing Gala attended by the Royal family. The event is held in the Fontvielle quarter in Monaco under a traditional circus big top.

The Folie Russe dancers were always invited to dance at the gala and it was truly an honour.

We danced for the entire Royal family at the time and at the end of our performance all made a deep curtsey to Prince Rainier, Prince Albert, Princess Caroline and Princess Stephanie.

Being Given the Axe

Around 4 weeks before the end of my contract, J.C. the head dancer called me in for a meeting at the end of the show. Very quickly and abruptly she told me that my contract was not being renewed, because, as she put it, "The management had decided that despite me being an excellent dancer, I had unfortunately gained too much weight and didn't look right next to the other dancers."

I was absolutely devastated. I went home and cried my eyes out. I felt totally humiliated.

Of course, I knew that I had put on some weight, the never-ending partying and socialising had taken its toll. I did not have any weighing scales at home but my clothes and costumes were feeling tighter, but for a professional dancer, even a few pounds are too much.

I have often looked back now and wondered why, as head dancer J.C. did not warn me earlier about my weight? Then I could have acted upon it.

On subsequent contracts we were weighed weekly and if anyone appeared to be gaining any weight, they were told *quickly* to do something about it and it was also written into our contracts that our weight should not increase by more than 4 pounds.

Another French dancer Corinne was also told the same fate and that her contract was not being renewed. She didn't seem too bothered and said in her cute French accent, "Bah! Well at least I can say I 'ave been one of Les Doriss Girls, I will always 'ave zis on my dancers CV forever, I deedd it."

It was the end of April and I made the most of my last few days In Monaco, spending as much time as I could with my dear friend Julie and walking the streets and taking in the historic beauty. The Grand Prix was soon to be there where the streets are turned into the racetrack and huge seating areas were being erected along the streets for the spectators. Day by day I would turn a different street corner that I could usually walk down and was no longer able to because the transformation had already started to take place for the race in May.

I wasn't sure where I wanted to try and go to work next, but I quickly contacted a few agents asking for work and fortunately was offered a contract in Mallorca, Spain starting straight after the end of my Monaco contract ended. It was a small touring show, I wasn't overly excited but I needed to work and loved Spain so I accepted the contract, while trying to starve myself.

My First Cigarette

I also decided that I should take up smoking, practically all the other dancers smoked and claimed that it helped them to stay thin, instead of eating they would smoke. I went to the local shop and bought a packet of cigarettes and a lighter and then went back to my studio and sat on the balcony trying to smoke my first cigarette aged 19!

I had never been tempted to smoke before, even when there was peer pressure at school to be in the 'smoking gang I just was not interested.

"Ugggh this is disgusting," I thought. I hated the taste and did not know how to inhale either so was coughing and spluttering. Ill keep practicing I decided, it's worth it if I can be thinner.

Monaco had been a crazy whirlwind. I had more than made up for the lack of social life that I had experienced in Paris.

I don't have many photos from my time in Monaco, I destroyed most of my photos because each time I looked at them I felt fat and ugly and I felt as though I had failed myself.

As I have grown older and wiser, I believe that 'Failure' is giving up without learning anything, so now I don't see that it was a failure, because in Monaco I did learn a lot, about a lot!

I was not overweight at all for a regular person. The harsh reality is that as a dancer, every inch of your body is under permanent scrutiny and it's your job to try and be physically perfect.

I Left Monaco and headed home to the UK via Paris, which gave me the opportunity to catch up very briefly with my dearest Liz aka Betty Buttocks, who was loving life as a Crazy Horse girl.

Back in the UK, it was always great to see my family. My youngest brother Chalky loved his bright red Ferrari F1 driving suit that Id bought him from Monaco and wore it nonstop. Mum and Dad had moved into a new home and allocated me a pretty, pink bedroom overlooking the front of the house, where I used to lean out of the window secretly practicing my smoking.

**PARIS, LA NOUVELLE EVE, CHEEKY *CANCAN* GIRLS,
WITH LIZ AKA BETTY BUTTOCKS**

EIFFEL TOWER: (L-R) ELAINE, AUNTY JEAN, ME, & MUM

BACKSTAGE, LA NOUVELLE EVE, PARIS

RED & SILVER COSTUMES, LA NOUVELLE EVE, PARIS

FAMILY DINNER: (L-R) GAYNOR, ADEY, MUM, DAD, & LITTLE BROTHER CHALKY NIGHT BEFORE MONACO CONTRACT WITH THE PAINTING I BOUGHT BACK

MONACO CARS ROUTINE BACKSTAGE WITH SOME OF THE CAST

SALOON GIRLS, MONACO: NICKI, GAYNOR, & AMANDA

CHAPTER SIX

Mallorca (Majorca)

MY ADDRESS

Calle Mendez Nunez, No 8, C'an Picafort, Mallorca

After only 3 days at home, I was on my way to my next dancing contract in Mallorca as it is spelt in Spain or Majorca as the British spell it. I travelled up to Manchester airport and met the other dancers from the show as we boarded our flight to Palma. It was raining as we took off from Manchester, but the sun was shining as we landed in beautiful Mallorca and were met by our boss, Tolo. We were taken to the small village of C'an Picafort on the north coast of Mallorca where the company had rented an apartment for us all to live in. It was a simple but nice apartment with views from our bedroom over to the sea.

The company had asked Louise and myself to both be joint head girls and dance captains. Louise and I hit it off straight away and decided to share a room together, we became lifelong friends and we have shared each others lives ever since, she is a genuine friend who I think the world of.

Lou had been dancing in Italy for a few years and only weeks before had the most awful heartbreaking experience. She was living in Southern

Italy, engaged to be married to an Italian man and in the process of setting up her own dancing school, when he ended up dying following a fatal car accident.

I though that she was being very brave coming out here to dance on another contract and also thought that it was probably the best thing to throw herself into something new to distract herself from her grief.

Rehearsals started the following morning and our choreographer; Aida who was originally from Belgium came to meet us all. We all jumped into a hire car and went the short distance to a little village hall where we were to rehearse.

To be honest I felt quite disorientated the first few days. I felt like my head was still in Monaco, with my body in a new place, Mallorca. I missed Julie and wasn't excited about the new contract so far.

I went into a restaurant about 10 days into my Mallorca contract and there on the TV was showing the Monaco Grand Prix. My heart skipped a beat. Just over two weeks ago I had still been there!

I called Julie from a payphone and it was wonderful to hear her news. I never actually saw Julie again though. We kept in touch for a few years exchanging letters but since we were constantly moving around the world it was quite hard and Julie went back to Wales I heard and gave up dancing. I have searched many times for her on the Internet but to no avail. Plus, if she married, her surname would have no doubt changed from Martin to something else. Julie if by some miracle you ever see this book, please get in touch with me through Facebook or Instagram.

The Mallorca show was a huge bump down to earth compared to any other shows that I had so far been lucky enough to work in. The costumes were low budget in comparison, rather like the kind of thing I used to wear in my dancing school shows. Gone were the fabulous feathers and head-dresses of Spain, Paris and Monaco. Since this was a travelling show, which basically meant damn hard work, running from hotel to hotel to perform our show, jumping back in the minivan and then racing to the next Hotel to repeat it, all of the costumes needed to be practical and very easy to throw into a bag and rush off to the next venue, there were no such luxuries as permanent dressing rooms, where feathers hung on walls and dressers and stage hands rushed to help dress us. Now we were getting changed in back rooms, cupboards, offices or toilets, wherever there was space to use as a makeshift changing room. I hated having to pack up my costumes quickly in a bag and rush to the next venue.

The show itself though was clever and entertaining. The Hotels in Mallorca were full of tourists from lots of different countries, so the show needed to work in any language, it was fast paced and visual and the music spoke to everyone in all languages as music does. We had dance routines to songs by Michael Jackson, Marilyn Monroe, The Andrew sisters boogie woogie number, a circus clown routine, which all of the kids loved, some breakdancing by the male dancer and of course a fabulous French cancan finale with audience participation. We would grab unsuspecting men from the audience, throw a frilly cancan skirt on them and they would join us in a final cancan kick line. Our changes were unbelievably fast since there were only five of us in the show and it was non-stop from start to finish. I had a solo to a Marilyn Monroe number where I was miming singing to "My heart belongs to Daddy," I wore a red sequin dress with a big white feather boa and shimmied around and high kicked my way through the routine and would throw my feather boa around the neck of some poor unsuspecting male in the audience and sit on his knee. These were family shows, so all very innocent and fun and the kids loved it if it was their Dad who was chosen to be embarrassed by Marilyn Monroe aka me.

One night, the other performers were all going out for food, but I had a bad headache and decided to stay at the apartment. I went into the lounge area and opened the cupboard doors of the sideboard, inside there was a stash of glossy magazines, in Spanish. Great I thought, I can understand most of it, and it will be good practice for me to start reading Spanish again after my last two contracts mostly speaking French.

I started flicking through the Spanish equivalent of *HELLO* magazine called *HOLA* and imagine my shock when I saw a photo of Christophe from Monaco. I quickly started to read the article trying as best as I could to translate and decipher it. It basically was telling the very story that I had been told about Christophe by the other dancers when I first arrived at the Folie Russe. Sure enough it said that he was the now disgraced, best friend of Prince Albert and he had been charged with possession of drugs and gave details about his prison sentence that he was beginning to serve. Lucky escape I reminded myself and tore out and kept the article intending to send it to Julie, which I forgot to do, so I still have it.

We had a local driver called Guillermo, which translates to William in English, so he told us to call him Will. He drove the tour bus and helped us set up our backdrop on the stage and organized the music for us. He seemed nice enough but we soon realised he would tell tales and snitch about us to the boss, Tolo.

Lou and I made our own friends outside of the show. Our shows were finished early most nights, since they were targeted at families. Almost every night after the shows, we would go to a nearby club in the next town of Alcudia, which was about a 20-minute drive away. The club was called Menta. This was a really cool club and we soon became good friends with everyone there.

The club had lots of different areas, there was a huge dance floor obviously in the main area surrounded by bars and then up some steps at the back was another open air bar and a huge swimming pool with a slide. The first time Lou and I visited there we both discussed the pool and said *who could be bothered to get all wet and go swimming on a night out?* Very soon afterwards though, we became regulars in the pool and realised just how great it was on the hot Spanish summer nights, all we needed was a swimsuit and a towel stashed away in the car. There was also a lovely out-door terrace area in a garden for drinks and snacks, where we often used to grab a ham and cheese toasty to refuel ourselves.

Lou and I started to jump up on the big music speakers and use them to dance on like podiums either side of the dance floor; we loved it and so did the club managers. Looking back, I like to think that Lou and I actually *invented* podium dancing.

I started to date one of the club owners, a local called Mateos. It wasn't a big love story but we enjoyed each other's company and had a mutual respect for each other, plus I enjoyed the stability and security after my disastrous Monaco relationships. Sometimes Mateo and I went down to Palma to other clubs and for dinner. The nightclub owners would often visit each other's clubs and exchange 'gifts' of cocaine, which was easy to access and always on the menu in Mallorca if you could afford it. I wasn't interested in cocaine myself, cigarettes, alcohol and cheese and ham toasties kept me happy.

Menta also did themed nights too and by this time we were such good friends with all the promo staff and team, that Lou and I actually got paid to come dressed in togas and be part of the floor show dancing around like Greek Goddesses, we were so pleased with the extra money, since we were really paid very low wages in Majorca, it was always a struggle to manage till the next pay day.

On the way back after the Greek Toga themed night, our car broke down. Lou was driving as usual she hardly ever drank alcohol and would perhaps have one alcohol drink per night and the rest of the time soft drinks and we had to wait for the police to rescue us and organise lifts home for us dressed in our togas! Of all the nights to break down we still laugh about it to this day.

We hardly ever ate at home, preferring to eat at all the restaurants along the beachfront filled with holidaymakers. It was a lovely atmosphere in C'an Picafort because everyone was on holiday and seemed happy. Lou did cook a couple of times though and made a fantastic Bolognaise, having lived in Italy for quite some time she was something of an expert and she was the one who taught me to cook pasta and bolognaise. Thank you, Lou.

Lou's Mum and Dad came to visit and we had a lovely week with them, visiting different beaches and villages of Mallorca. I wished that my parents had visited me. I knew that Mum would always want to, but Dad didn't facilitate it. Not for the first time, I thought how nice it must be to have the sort of parents who came together to visit and stayed in an Hotel or apartment for a week to visit me, see the show that I was performing in while making a holiday of it as lots of the other dancers parents did.

As usual my big brother Adey came to visit though, it was all very short notice and since we did not have a phone in our apartment, he wasn't able to phone ahead, so imagine my surprise when I returned to the apartment to find Adey and his friend Steve standing on my balcony waving to me. He had met the other dancers who were at home and they had let him in. What a great surprise.

At the end of the Mallorca contract our boss offered some of us the chance to carry on with the same show but in the Canary Islands for the winter season in Lanzarote.

I decided that I would accept the job offer, I liked the sound of the climate in The Canary Islands and fancied a warm winter and I simply didn't fancy the hassle of trekking up and down to London for auditions.

Mateo and I said our farewells but neither of us pretended that we were heartbroken or that we would try to meet up again very soon. We had enjoyed a fun summer romance together.

Lou decided that she wanted to go back to work in Italy or elsewhere, we said sad goodbyes at the airport as we went home our separate ways. I went back to Stoke-on-Trent for a very short stay and then jetted off to start the new contract in Lanzarote.

CHAPTER SEVEN

Lanzarote

MY ADDRESS

Tabaybas, apt D2, Avenida de Las Playas, Puerto Del Carmen

Once again, I found myself taking off from rainy Manchester airport and landing to hot sun, this time in Arrecife, the capital of Lanzarote.

As soon as I arrived in Lanzarote, I decided I liked it.

Lanzarote is a beautiful volcanic Canary Island. Filled with palm trees, whitewashed abodes, white apartments, white Hotels, white restaurants, beautiful and interesting beaches and lots of cacti. I loved this clean, stark whiteness contrasting against the very hot blue-sky backdrop and palm trees.

The other dancers arrived and we started rehearsals, it was quite a nice relaxed rehearsal period since I already knew most of the choreography. I enjoyed getting to know the other dancers who were frantically trying to learn all of the dance routines. During rehearsals, we lived in holiday apartments 'Cinco Plazas' Hotel in Puerto Del Carmen, which was the main busy, buzzing holiday destination in Lanzarote. We loved it here being right in the centre of Puerto Del Carmen with shops, the beach, restaurants and nightclubs all nearby.

I very quickly became friendly with Dawn, one of the other dancers and we shared a room together. One day Dawn and I walked along the seafront to the supermarket to buy our food groceries; it was so hot walking back that we left our shopping bags on the rocks for 5 minutes and jumped in the sea for a quick swim to cool off, we always had swim wear on under a pair of shorts or sundress. How great, we thought, we certainly wouldn't be stripping off and jumping in the sea in UK in November on our way back from the supermarket. These privileges were some of the things that made our lives and jobs so fun.

Once rehearsal period was over, we had to move to a different apartment that our boss had organized further out of Puerto Del Carmen in a small sleepy village called Tias. This was an hour-long walk away involving lots of hills or 15 minutes in a taxi. There was practically no public transport and obviously being 20 years old we wanted to go out after the show every night in this fun holiday island where everyone was out partying on holiday.

Dawn and I couldn't afford taxis every night and it was not always easy to find one, so one night, we decided to hitchhike. After a few minutes a man aged around 40 pulled up and said he was going that way. He was local but spoke a little English; my Spanish was pretty good so I chatted to him a bit being polite. When he pulled over to let us get out of the car, Dawn who was in the front got out first and as I got out from the back seat, he decided to put his hand up my skirt and was grabbing and stroking my bottom, putting his hand inside my underwear. I was furious; I whacked him with my handbag, called him something very rude in Spanish and slammed his car door.

As soon as I got home I jumped in the shower to cleanse myself from his disgusting wandering hands.

I felt dirty. We never hitchhiked again.

The only good thing about that incident was that it made us decide to talk to our bosses and say we needed an apartment in the centre of Puerto Del Carmen, otherwise we were refusing to do any more shows. They quickly agreed and told us to find one and set a budget. Within 24 hours we had found one and moved in.

Now that we were based back in Puerto Del Carmen, we were much happier and went out most nights after we finished our shows. It was a fantastic atmosphere in Puerto Del Carmen since almost everyone there was on holiday and happy. Dawn and I went into a busy and bustling cocktail bar called Paradise and the manager got chatting to us asking if we were enjoying our holiday. We explained to him that we were professional dancers living here and had our shows to perform in.

He asked if we would be interested in coming to Paradise after our Hotel shows finished and dance in the DJ box along with the D.J. in a raised stage area in the centre of the club. We negotiated a fee and of course free drinks and we had ourselves a deal.

From then on, Dawn and I would finish our hotel shows at around 10 p.m. and head down to Paradise, which was just opening for the night, and help with the partying, dancing around with tambourines and maracas, we loved it.

We used to pick our outfits to wear from our own wardrobe, we went and bought some cute matching outfits because we wanted to look professional and not look like two girls who had just jumped into the DJ box by accident. Our friends would come into Paradise and hang out with us too. We were doubling our wages and obviously very happy about that.

On our third night, Tony the manager told us to smile and dance our best since the owner, Fernando, was back from holiday and would be in tonight. Fernando owned numerous restaurants, bars and nightclubs on the Island. On one of our drinks breaks, Tony asked us to come over and meet Fernando, he introduced us to him and his girlfriend. Fernando was very friendly and invited us to have drinks with them; we joined them for a quick drink and then thanked them and said we must return to the D.J. box stage since we were being paid to keep the holidaymakers partying.

Once Dawn and I finished our DJ box dancing, we would go next door, downstairs underground to an amazing nightclub called Joker, which was also owned by Fernando. Joker was the most fashionable and largest nightclub in Puerto Del Carmen at that time. The whole back wall of this club was a huge aquarium, I often wondered whether the fish liked the music or not blasting out, but they certainly seemed happy enough.

On the door along with the security was a little dwarf guy dressed up in a Joker outfit, everyone wanted photos with him, what a fun job. In the daytime he would walk along the beach with the promotion team and give out flyers for Joker, telling people what was going to be happening that night at the club.

Fernando came into Paradise almost every night, sometimes with his girlfriend and other nights without her. He told me that they had always had an arrangement that they could do their own thing on the nights that they did not see each other, I thought that was all a bit strange. They had been in a relationship for many years but did not live together. He was always surrounded by girls, charming them with his wit and flirting.

When we finished dancing in Paradise at around midnight, he would often invite us and our friends to join him in Joker for drinks. For Dawn and me that was when we relaxed because as fun as all our dancing was, be it in the *Moonlight Stars* Hotel shows or the DJ box at Paradise, we were still on duty and smiling, we needed to wind down and switch off at bit before we headed home to bed. We had the whole day to sleep, swim and sunbathe such was our dancers life.

The following week, Fernando invited Dawn and me to go for lunch with him.

We agreed and stood outside of our apartment keen not to be late for the boss and he collected us in his gold convertible Jaguar and took us to a typical Canarian restaurant beside the sea for freshly caught fish, *lenguado* which is plaice in English.

I can honestly say that the fish in El Golfo in Lanzarote is the best I ever tasted. The fish was always freshly caught and served with two sauces called *MOJO* in Spanish, a red mojo and a green mojo. These *mojos* were typical Canarian sauces, consisting of an olive oil base, peppers, and various spices such as garlic and paprika. Every Canarian family has its own secret recipe for mojo, so it can vary in spiciness and texture. They are absolutely delicious as an accompaniment to the fresh fish with local *patatas arrugadas,* which means wrinkled potatoes. Due to the volcanic land, the potatoes grown in Lanzarote were really small sized because of the lack of water, around the size of a small plum with thick skins. These potatoes would be scrubbed and cooked in boiling salty water until the water evaporated and the potatoes had salty wrinkly skins. They tasted delicious.

These fresh, simple lunches served with ice cold white wine were delicious and some of the best food I have ever eaten anywhere, sat outside in the sun, with sea spray on your cheeks while devouring the fresh fish and watching the sea waves smashing on to the rocks. It really was paradise.

It was now December and The following week, Fernando invited Dawn and I out to lunch again and this time we went to a beach to cook paella. To get to the beach we had to go off road over a lot of sand dunes, passing camels and then walk the last little bit to the pebble beach. He set up the Paella dish over a small gas burner and started to cook the paella, once all the ingredients were in, it needed to cook for another 30 minutes or so, so we all did what we always did in Lanzarote and jumped in the sea for a swim. When the paella was cooked, we ate it straight out of the paellera dish and drank crisp cold wine that he had brought in a cool box. The combination of the sea right next to us and the sun made it all seem wonderful, how lucky I was to be living this wonderful life as a dancer, travelling the world, experiencing new adventures all whilst being paid to do something that I loved.

At the end of the meal, Fernando gave Dawn and I small presents wrapped in Christmas paper, he told us to open them now since he was going away for a couple of weeks with his girlfriend and wouldn't be back until after New Year. Dawn went first and had a lovely pair of large gold earrings and I opened mine and it was a beautiful gold necklace with a heart on it. I remember blushing and thinking, I think he likes me, I liked him too, but the problem was, he already had a long-term girlfriend.

On Christmas day, Dawn and I went down to the beach and swam and sunbathed and then had a barbeque lunch, we went to phone boxes and phoned our families to wish them a Happy Christmas, and while they were huddled around fires, we were huddled around barbeques on the beach, sunbathing and swimming, how amazing it was to be able to experience such a different Christmas. Last year I had been in Monaco and this year I was sunbathing on a beach with Dawn.

We headed off to do our two shows of course, there never any days off for us obviously, we were here to entertain the lucky holidaymakers who had chosen a hot and sunny holiday for Christmas.

Fuerteventura

As well as performing in Lanzarote we were also contracted to go over to the neighbouring island of Fuerteventura every two weeks for a couple of nights to do shows on that island.

Fuerteventura means 'strong winds' in Spanish and this island was appropriately named. The island is absolutely stunning; it is the second largest Canary Island in size, however it is much quieter with less people and hotels than the other Islands. It has beautiful beaches, sand dunes and mountains all within this unique and beautiful island. The majority of visitors seemed to be either windsurfers due to the intense wind and big waves, couples, or families with very young children; this definitely was not a party Island area.

I loved our trips to Fuerteventura because it was really quite an adventure. We took a small ferry from Lanzarote over to Fuerteventura which landed in Corralejo, a beautiful fishing village which was now slowly turning into a holiday village and then we drove in our tour minibus to the Jandia Sol hotel where we stayed and performed. The accommodation for us entertainers was a very large room with lots of bunk beds and two bathrooms. We had great fun all sleeping in the big room together; it was like doing a big sleepover with all your friends.

Sometimes when we had family visiting, they came with us to Fuerteventura and there were enough bunk beds in the room for them to all stay too. My mum, aunty Jean my Godmother and my young brother Chalky all came together to visit me in Lanzarote and they loved the Fuerteventura adventure of the ferry and the bunk beds.

The other attraction in Fuerteventura was for nudists we found out. The staff at the hotel told us that nudism was allowed in Fuerteventura which makes it really popular with naturalists who want to enjoy a private and relaxed naked day at the beach. Dawn and I had never experienced a nudist beach so we decided that we would go and check it out. We were used to sunbathing topless anyway, since we were not allowed to get any sun tan strap marks.

So off we went in search of a nudist beach, there was one very nearby and it was full of older visitors particularly from Scandinavian countries and Germany who all came here because they liked the nudist beaches. Dawn and I set out our towels and lay down on the beach, we had our small bikini thongs on, but I just did not feel comfortable to remove my thong, even though we were the only ones on the whole beach with a stitch of clothing on and stitch is an appropriate word because our sunbathing thongs were literally a small triangle of fabric at the front and then thin string around the back, again so that we did not incur strap lines or tan lines. We both were trying not to giggle too loudly when all of the people, especially the old men, were trotting around the beach with their bits and bobs swinging and bouncing around!

On one occasion our choreographer Aida decided to come over with us to watch the shows and make sure everything was in order, she brought her little dog with her. She absolutely adored her little dog, we all did. At one point, she asked us to look after the dog while she went to speak to the management and off she went. So we were all sitting around on our bunk beds looking after the gorgeous little dog he was playing with us and then having cuddles on the top bunk with Dawn. Suddenly for some reason he decided to do a great big leap and jumped off the bed landing head down on the hard floor. I was lying in my bunk bed next door on the bottom level and saw this all happen, it always seems like slow motion when its something awful happening, even though it was all in a split second. We were horrified we looked down at the floor so scared and upset. Had the bosses dog just been killed while in our care?! The dog lay there not moving for what seemed like an eternity, in reality it was probably only a few seconds of concussion, thankfully within a few more seconds which seemed like a lifetime, the dog got up and walked across the room back to normal we were so relieved.

The other thing that stayed clearly in my mind about Fuerteventura was the amount of cockroaches that seemed to be everywhere, obviously there were cockroaches in Lanzarote too, but not the amount that seemed to be in Fuerteventura, it felt like the cockroach headquarters of the world.

One night after finishing our show, we decided to go the hotel nightclub for some drinks and a dance, we were always given free drinks. I decided to get up and have a bit of a dance with Dawn and we couldn't believe it, there were loads of cockroaches running around the dance floor. Who knew that cockroaches liked clubbing and dancing too? The holidaymakers and us tried to avoid standing on them, we had all had a few cocktails so it seemed funny.

Once when we were over in Fuerteventura, I headed to the bar to get a diet coke after our show and a girl came rushing over to say hello to me, it was only Mandy again! *The* same Mandy that I had met on the coach at Birmingham airport, on my way to my first job in Spain. Neither of us could believe it and were so happy to bump into each other again. Mandy was on holiday with her fiancé, they had just got engaged. It was surreal bumping into her like that, in a remote hotel in Fuerteventura. I love those coincidences in life.

Although we enjoyed our Fuerteventura gigs, we were always happy to get back to Lanzarote after 2 nights and be back with all of our friends and the party scene of Lanzarote.

We were over in Fuerteventura for our last performances of the year, when the weather suddenly turned violently bad. Our ferry back was cancelled and there were no flights either. We were stranded in Corralejo. There was nothing we could do, so we went to dinner and all went to sleep in a small accommodation that we had found near to the harbour expecting that the weather would improve when we woke up the next day. Unfortunately, it was actually even worse. Once again all the ferries were cancelled and it was now December 30th. We were all panicking we just wanted to get back to Lanzarote. While we were stuck there, Tolo our boss sent us to a hotel that night where there were supposed to be some magicians performing who were stuck in Lanzarote. We were hoping and praying that the weather would improve because the following day was December 31st and we were desperate to be back in Lanzarote with our friends.

The following morning the weather had not changed, there were still no ferries and no flights. Down at the harbor we chatted to some locals who offered to take us back to Lanzarote on their small sailing boat. They were very confident and they said that without a doubt they could make it, they had sailed through worse than this.

We called our boss who agreed to pay the fees, because he wanted us back to do our shows for New Year's Eve. We all boarded the small yacht, there were other locals telling us not to go. "You are absolutely crazy." There was even one old local Spanish lady crying as we set off. I felt as though I was in a bad film, but young, fearless (and stupid), we all agreed we wanted to give it a go.

This was like nothing else that I have ever experienced and I never want to experience again in my life. Within minutes I was throwing up over the side of the yacht, smashing against the waves. I decided to stumble inside downstairs and lie down. I could not speak; I could not move, it was horrendous all I could hear and feel were the crashing waves. I don't know how long passed, then suddenly I heard lots of shouting and commotion upstairs that didn't sound good, everyone was sounding upset and annoyed. The mainsail had ripped, due to the extremely high winds and was broken and we now had to turn around and head *back* to Fuerteventura. The thought of having to endure this dreadful journey again, only to end up back in Fuerteventura was painful.

I remember seeing the face of our formerly very confident Captain and he now looked afraid. God and the angels were on our side and we arrived back in Corralejo.

Arrangements were quickly made with our bosses and we were sent to an hotel to perform again, filling in for the magicians who were still stuck in Lanzarote. When midnight rolled around it was not the New Years Eve that any of us had hoped for, but we were grateful that we were alive at least.

Happily and safely back in Lanzarote a few days later, we arrived at Paradise when Tony called me over.

"Sorry, you are fired, you can't dance here anymore."

"Why?" I asked.

"Fernando's orders. That's all I know and if you want to speak to him, he will be in the office downstairs in Joker and said only Gaynor to go."

Dawn was happy with that since I was older than her and the dance captain. "He obviously likes you so you might have a better chance of winning him over," she said.

I went into the office fired up and ready to fight our corner, we still had our Moonlight Stars show jobs, but we liked our extra money and free drinks for a couple of hours dancing around in Paradise so I wanted to know what had brought this on.

Fernando was sitting behind his desk smiling; I smiled back and wished each other a Happy New Year. Then I asked why he no longer wanted us to dance at Paradise. He said, "Well, I have decided that I want you to be my girlfriend."

Fernando said that since I was now going to be his girlfriend—in his arrogant and confident manner—he didn't want his girlfriend to dance at Paradise and instead wanted me to be able to be with him, at his side. I asked him what had happened with him and his girlfriend and he said that they were no longer together but gave no further details. I later heard from a friend of hers that I was apparently "the last straw" she had become tired of his wandering eye, after years of him being unfaithful to her and no commitment.

I asked if Dawn could keep her job if she wanted to, why should she lose out? To which he agreed. Dawn didn't stay working there long though, without me around Tony kept hitting on her and because she wasn't interested in him, he then became mean to her.

At the beginning of the relationship, I loved being Fernando's girlfriend at that time, he was fun to be around and our lifestyle was glamourous and exhilarating. He lavished attention on me and was very romantic. We frequented his restaurants and nightclubs after the shows and obviously we always had the best table in the house and his staff treated us like royalty, since he was the boss. One night we were in a nightclub that he owned in Costa Teguise and there were Spanish ladies that walked around the clubs selling fresh red roses at extortionate prices. He made the rose seller very happy, by buying me the whole basket of roses as we were on our way out leaving the club. He was often flirty with other girls though which annoyed me, inviting them to join us for drinks when we were out, so that our romantic evening for two then turned into a completely different evening, with a harem of pretty girls! He always just said that he was a nightclub owner and it went with his job.

When Mum, Aunty Jean and Chalky came over to visit me in Lanzarote, I was so excited having them there and Fernando and I showed them all around the Island. We took them to many beautiful places of interest in Lanzarote such as, Timanfaya National Park, which looks like a moonscape from a film and is home to dormant volcanoes that last erupted in 1824.

At the Montanas Del Fuego centre (meaning mountains of fire) there is a restaurant where the food is cooked using the natural geothermal heat.

A highlight that we still laugh about is the camel rides that we all took; Aunty Jean was hilarious on her camel. We mounted the camels when they were seated on the floor so when they start to stand up, its important to lean back to avoid landing headfirst in the sand, which Aunty Jean didn't quite do, there was lots of shrieking and loud shouts of "*Oops-a-daisy*" from Aunty Jean, one of her favourite expressions. Miraculously she managed to stay on the camel with a few sharp pushes from the cameleer men. Once you are on the camel, the views are beautiful since you are high up and the side-to-side rocking sensation is quite relaxing. The camels made us laugh too with their snorting and face pulling, they are beautiful creatures and have their own unique personalities, making them very easy to love, but they can kick in all four directions too with each of their legs, so watch out!

A highlight for my younger brother Chalky was seeing the tiny albino crabs glistening in the water at The Jameos Del Agua. This is a beautiful tranquil place where due to an underground volcanic eruption a magical series of lava caves were formed, with openings to the sky. It is in the north of Lanzarote and there were hundreds of the tiny crabs that are blind.

Mum, Chalky and Aunty Jean all piled into the tour bus with us and loved watching the shows and seeing the different Hotels where we toured and performed.

The end of our contract came around quickly and our boss did not have any more contracts in Lanzarote since he would be taking the show to re start in Mallorca again soon for the summer season and there weren't any other shows to audition for in Lanzarote. Fernando invited me to stay on after the end of my contract and organised an apartment for me opposite the beach near to his office.

Without my shows to perform now, we did not need to be out at nighttime and enjoyed hanging out at his home a lot. We had a happy period enjoying doing day to day things, like taking the dogs for walks around the rugged terrain where he lived and picked fresh cockles and mussels from the rocks and cooked them in garlic. We even painted his swimming pool on the inside, blue obviously and it took several days and lots of scrubbing for the little specks of paint to disappear from our skin since it was after all waterproof and swimming pool paint.

I knew that I would have to start thinking about my next dancing job soon and Fernando was planning to leave Lanzarote and sail around the world indefinitely. He talked excitedly about this and his sailing boat that was being built near to Barcelona. I really could not bear the thought of a sad and awkward goodbye; I had fallen in love with him.

I waited until I knew that he was away on business for a few days and planned to leave the day before he returned and leave him a card thanking him for the nice times we had shared. I walked to a travel agency and bought my plane ticket home to the UK.

Early the next morning, I went to his empty office and saw his secretary, in her office next door. Renata had been a girlfriend of Fernando's, which resulted in them having a son together. Although they did not stay in a relationship, he did provide for their son and had offered her a job as his secretary, which worked well. I liked Renata. She was German and always kind and friendly to me. When their son, who was around 7 years old at that time, spent time with us, I used to enjoy playing with him and I think she appreciated the effort that I made with him. I waved to her and we exchanged pleasantries. I left the farewell card on his desk and went back to my room and started packing for the evening flight, feeling desperately sad.

Shortly afterwards, there was a knock at the door. Imagine my surprise, it was Fernando. He had come back a day early! He was holding my opened card in his hand and simply said, "What's this?"

He invited me for lunch and when we got there asked to see my plane ticket, which I was keeping in my handbag for safety. When I handed it to him, he ripped it up and said he did not want me to leave and to come and stay at his villa with him! I couldn't believe it and was ecstatically happy.

His beautiful villa was in a remote area and since I did not have a driving license, Fernando got me a moped to use. I loved the freedom of driving around on that and feeling independent if he was busy at the office, it stopped me being stuck out at home which was very isolated.

At the villa, there were lots of animals, which I loved. There were several dogs, chickens, several exotic birds including two beautiful large Macaw parrots called Azul (blue) and Rojo (red) who both spoke very well and clearly, they had been taught lots of funny expressions and rude swear words.

Bullet in My Leg

There was also a glass house with a pond in where turtles and a Pet baby crocodile lived. Fernando would hunt little birds for the crocodile to eat, one day I was sunbathing lying on my front reading a book when I heard Fernando using his BB gun to hunt small birds for the crocodile. Nothing unusual there, except suddenly I felt a sharp pain in my left ankle, he had shot me in the ankle by mistake. To this day I never really understood how that happened—surely if he was aiming at a bird anywhere near to me, he should have shouted up for me to move for a few minutes? Anyway the stupid idiot did not, so I ended up with a bleeding ankle. I hobbled inside and he helped me clean up the wound, the bullet appeared to have skimmed the skin and taken a layer off, so we patched it up and it healed within a week or so. Unbeknownst to me at that time, the bullet was actually lodged inside my leg!

We travelled to Gran Canaria, Madrid and Barcelona for holidays and went to see the *SCALA* shows. The Scala shows were the Spanish equivalent of The Moulin Rouge, at the time they owned three magnificent shows in Spain, Scala Madrid, Scala Barcelona and Scala Gran Canaria. It was wonderful to be back in Madrid and imagine my surprise when the show started and I spotted my dear friend Aldo on the stage, he spotted me too I could tell and we grinned from ear to ear at each other, him on the stage and me in the audience. At the end of the show the waiters came over and gave me a message that we were invited back stage by Aldo and went upstairs to the dressing rooms and met some of the cast. Aldo told me they needed dancers since a few were leaving soon.

When I returned to Lanzarote, since I knew that Fernando would be leaving soon on his boat, I put the wheels in motion to go to Scala Madrid. By this point my CV was good enough to not need to audition, any prospective employers could see from the caliber of shows that I had already danced in that I was obviously a good dancer, the only thing that needed to be checked was our weight and measurements, so we had to send in current photos of ourselves with our statistics. Christina Riba who was the boss of the prestigious Scala shows responded quickly offering me a place in the Madrid show, which I accepted.

Fernando then asked me to join him sailing. We discussed the adventure and the plan was I would take the contract and go to Scala Madrid, he would be based in Barcelona where the shipbuilding yard was and oversee his yacht being built and we would meet up in Madrid and Barcelona.

Once his boat was finished and he had sailed successfully across the Atlantic, Id fly out and meet him in the Caribbean and we would sail around the world together.

I was beyond excited.

After a quick stopgap visit back to the UK to see my parents, I was on my way to Madrid to join the show.

CHAPTER EIGHT

Scala Madrid

MY ADDRESS

Calle Rosario Pino 12, No 185, 28020, Madrid

was super excited to be joining the cast of Scala Madrid and dancing with Aldo again.

I had always kept in touch with my friends Catarina and Miguel and when they heard that I was coming to work back in Madrid, they were happy and helpful. I stayed with them for a night and then I moved into Catarina's mum's apartment while I looked for an apartment or room.

We started our rehearsals with Fiona, the dance captain who was British.

Fiona had been there for several years and as well as being the dance captain she would still perform in the show, usually covering for the principal dancer Helen or one of the topless nudes. The other new dancer that joined at the same time as me was Rosie, aptly named because she truly was the epitome of a beautiful English rose; she had trained at the prestigious Bush Davies Academy. This was her first professional job but Rosie ticked all of the boxes to be a future principal dancer. We would rehearse together in the daytime and then sit on the balcony area and watch the show in the evening to get familiar and piece it all together in our heads as instructed by Fiona.

A couple of days into rehearsals, a friendly dancer called Sarah found me to say that she shared an apartment directly opposite the show and her room was a twin room with a spare bed if I was interested. I moved straight in to *Calle Rosario Pino, 12* with Sarah and two acrobats from one of the attractions in the show. Rosie also moved into the same building, sharing with another dancer from the show.

There were two tall, stunning, principal boy dancers, Wayne was dark and handsome and Philip was blonde and handsome. They were both from South Africa originally and had performed in the world class shows at Sun City. They seemed to be very competitive with each other, there was a lot of hostility between them which performing on stage together night after night seemed to intensify.

Philip had piercing blue eyes and a sharp clipped South African accent. There was always a queue of beautiful men who wanted to be his boyfriend. Backstage he was a huge diva, which I found entertaining and loved. We became good friends and I remember him helping me to practice my split jete jumps in the reception area during rehearsals. As well as being an outstanding dancer himself he was also a patient and wonderful teacher.

I couldn't believe my eyes a few years later, when I saw him on a TV show in the UK called *The Cruise* alongside Jane McDonald, he was being a big diva on screen, which I *could* believe.

Fernando and I spoke every day and he was eager to fly up to Madrid to see me. When he came to Madrid, he would book a room and we would stay in the Hotel where our show was, The Melia Castilla Hotel. This was wonderful and I felt very privileged to be living in the luxury of the Hotel.

When he needed to fly back to Lanzarote or Barcelona I would stay back in my twin room with Sarah.

One evening in rehearsal period, Rosie and I went over to a café opposite the stage door entrance for snacks and drinks in between the two shows. There was a British journalist there from *The Sun* newspaper asking questions about a tiger that was allegedly being kept in a cage backstage.

It was easy to spot the dancers since they all had their heavy showgirl make up on. No one seemed to want to talk to the journalist, but someone did. I thought it was a bit odd because there definitely was not a tiger in the show. It turned out to be true though. One of the stagehands asked if we would like to see the tiger and sure enough there was a big beautiful tiger in a cage backstage waiting to be taken to his next venue. He had been part of one of the attractions that had recently finished performing there before we arrived.

I felt so sad for the Tiger. A week or so later the story was part of the front page of *The Sun* newspaper.

The Scala Madrid show turned out to be my favourite show to dance in ever. There was no expense spared on this show. The costumes were magnificent as were the sets and hydraulic stage.

One of our routines was a tap routine where the whole back area of the stage raised up and became water fountains, and one of the male dancers, Les, would leap and jump spectacularly through the water with an umbrella, miming to "Singing in the Rain." The sound of the water was thunderous and very impressive the audiences loved it and there was cheering and clapping and *ooh-ing* and *aa-hing* There is nothing quite so magical as seeing the audience enthralled all smiling and clapping.

We had of course several talented attraction acts in this show.

One of the attractions was a stunning ice skating duo. Peter and Cynthia. An ice rink would rise up from under the stage and the couple performed beautiful and breathtaking ice-skating and acrobatics to rapturous applause. They would finish their act in the centre of the ice rink waving until they disappeared, as they slowly started to descend back down under the stage.

Another attraction, were three French Canadian acrobats called Men In Design, they were ex Olympic athletes who had now reinvented themselves as an acrobatic balancing act, touring shows worldwide. The money was far better they said than being athletes previously and they were making the most of it while their bodies held up.

My favourite attraction in the show was the spectacular Spanish Ballet. This was highly charged and was a fusion of modern and traditional Spanish flamenco dancing. The Andalucian music was dramatic, even if you didn't understand the words you could feel the deep emotion in your soul and with the heel stomping, hand clapping, castanets and shouts of "ole ole," it just took your breath away. The dancers were all Spanish and incredibly talented. We all became good friends and often socialized with them between the shows or afterwards.

My favourite dance routine that I performed was where there were only three of us dancers, the principal dancer, myself and one other who would all rise up from under the stage and appear in a beautiful shiny open top red sports car. We would sing and dance in, around and on top of the beautiful sports car, whilst Miguel one of the acrobats from the show, pretended to be a mechanic, flipping and somersaulting around the car and stage, flexing his muscles and flirting with us. We would all sing in Spanish about how much we loved going to the gym *'gimnasio'* while dancing on the seats and bonnet of the car and then jump out from the back seats of the car and slide down the boot of the car to the stage, kicking and dancing. It was so much fun and gave a little chance to be in the limelight for a few minutes and show a little of my own personality. There was a quick change before this routine, where I would have to run down lots of stairs to reach the area beneath the stage and we would crawl into the car and lie down until the stage above opened up and the car and us were raised up to audience level.

Vikings was probably the most dramatic and breathtaking number, we would make a dramatic entrance on a huge Viking ship that filled almost the width of the huge stage, slowly sailing on to the stage in a fog of sea mist (dry ice) to the dramatic theme tune from the movie *Raiders of the Lost Ark.*

Our female Viking outfits were sultry and we all looked like warrior princesses. The choreography for this routine was by Claudette Walker a well know French choreographer, who had also choreographed one of the routines in the Monaco show. At one point the male dancers would stand facing the audience with their legs astride and the female dancers had to turn and face the male dancers and do a handstand against the male dancers, who would catch the top of their legs and steady them against their shoulders, then they would reach down and lift the female dancers up away from the floor from behind their backs so that they were then sitting on the boys shoulders, with their crotches in the boys faces! Hmmm nice!

There was no expense spared backstage in this extravagant production either. We had the most wonderful seamstresses and dressers that we called *sastre* in Spanish. My favourite sastre was a gorgeous lady called Conchi who was there every night, they would repair immediately any rips in our costumes and even if we got a hole In our amazing fishnet tights, we would run up to the table and stick our leg or butt cheek in front of them and they would immediately repair our tights, as if by magic the former hole was now invisible. I was actually very good at repairing fishnet tights myself by now, I prided myself on this and obviously in most shows we had to do this ourselves. We were truly spoiled in this show and never had to do it ourselves.

The sastres and stage hands would also help us with quick changes, there were a few in this show that were virtually impossible, with less than a minute to be out of one costume and ready to run back on stage in the next.

The only way to make it was to be SUPER organized and not panic, just do what was required. We would run off stage and then they would unzip our costumes, quickly pulling them down over our hips or up over our heads as we stepped out of one and then stepped into the next costume laid out ready and the other person would already be pulling this up and zipping us into the next one and trying to balance whichever wig or headdress on to our heads. This was all while adding jewellery and gloves, and finally thrusting fans or Viking swords and other such accessories in to our hands as we ran back on stage.

I was always surprised and grateful that there were not more serious injuries. This show was fabulous, with the stage opening and closing, raising and swallowing ice rinks, cars fountains and staircases, but there was obviously a huge amount of danger involved if you were not in exactly the right place at the right time.

For our finale feather routine we would parade around a thin runway sized portion of stage, in our magnificent and heavy feather backpacks that lit up with big battery packs built in them all carefully hidden behind our backs and feathers. These backpacks were welded to steel frames and weighed around 40 pounds. Moving gracefully while wearing these, with heavy headdresses and high heels could be quite challenging, but we were not allowed to show this on our faces, it must be the signature beautiful showgirl smile.

There was a huge thirty foot hole drop directly behind us, from this hole would rise up beautifully lit, mirrored stair cases. I was at the front of my parading line and the first dancer that had to step from the runway strip on to the moving staircase over a large gap and the huge drop. *Mind the gap* took on a whole new meaning. It was crucial to step on to the staircase in our dancers heels at exactly the right time and there were ten other showgirls behind me waiting to get into their next position on the stage in split second time. Each night my heart would be in my mouth, thankfully I usually managed it bang on time and most importantly without incurring any injuries.

Fiona the dance captain ran a tight ship and each week did weekly weigh-ins. It was written in contracts that no one should gain more than 4 pounds in weight and could be dismissed if they did since they were in breach of their contract. It goes without saying though that due to the constant pressure to be thin there were many dancers that I knew with eating disorders.

For some reason, Fiona told me that I didn't need to do the weigh ins, I was exempt. I was very thin at this period in my life and pleased with this result, I thought back to Monaco and I felt pleased that I now seemed to be in control of my weight. Not that it was healthy in all honesty, I barely ate, I smoked lots, drank lots of coffee and lived off Marmite on toast, ham and cheese toasties or *sandwich mixtos* as they are called in Spain and bags of chocolate malteasers. If I was with Fernando, we ate in very nice restaurants nearby, often spying Julio Iglesias and other Spanish celebrities dining in the same places, we usually favoured fish restaurants, washed down with crisp white wine.

Some of the other dancers were struggling with weight maintenance, but by doing the weekly weigh in, it gave Fiona and them an opportunity to be completely aware of this and do something about it quickly and keep on top of it.

This was much better than what had happened to me in Monaco.

Laxatives were a popular remedy to try and keep the weight down. I tried these a few times but was never really convinced that I lost weight; I just seemed to spend more time in a toilet. Many of the girls were taking diet pills in Madrid and some were bulimic, throwing up after they ate in order to keep down their weight.

I loved being back in Madrid again, along with the other dancers after the shows, we regularly frequented *Joy Eslava* again, we only had to say that we were the dancers from Scala and we were always whisked through without having to queue. I often thought back to my first contract being there and remembered Lynda and me flushing the cocaine away in the toilet cubicle that the producer had given us!

The cast at Scala Madrid was from all over the world as usual, lots of South Africans, Canadians, British, German, Australian, and Spanish girls mainly. Directly behind me sat a stunning Argentinian dancer called Marina, who was an amazing dancer, friendly and smart. We would laugh and chat together, in both Spanish and English and of course my dear friend Aldo was here with me and it was such fun to be dancing together again. One evening Aldo and I made our way together over to the café bar that most people went to in between the shows for Coffee. When we got there we saw Alfredo, the very man and dancer who had collected me from the airport with Erin on my first dancing job for Ricardo Ferrante. Aldo and Alfredo started to chat; they obviously had known each other for several years and were fellow Argentinians. I said *hola* to Alfredo and walked slightly ahead as they were chatting away in Spanish. I knew that he would never remember me from those years back. Alfredo had just watched the show and I was flattered when I overheard Alfredo saying to Aldo, "And this girl, your friend here is phenomenal."

Those moments are special and memorable, when a highly respected and amazing dancer is complementing YOU. Thank you Alfredo.

We would all wander in and out of each other's dressing rooms, smoking and chatting when we had breaks while the attractions were on stage wowing the audiences.

A few months in some fun British dancers joined the show that I became friends with, Venetia, Nikki and Vicky. I had moved to another apartment with some other dancers a little further away, but the main attraction was the roof top swimming pool, which in Madrid in the summer was an absolute luxury. In the summertime, the weather was unbearably hot in the city with no sea breeze and as I walked to the show in the early evening I passed digital weather thermometers flashing up 40 degrees. When I was due to leave the show, Nikki who I nicknamed 'Pickle' decided to take over my room in the apartment that I was now sharing and for the last few weeks we shared my room together with a spare mattress on the floor. I have great memories of that fun time; we laughed so much I don't know how we ever found the time to sleep.

I also had my other friends outside of the show and caught up with Marta and Andresito again, which was great. My dear friends Catarina and Miguel announced that they were getting married and invited me to their wedding. I was honoured to attend such a beautiful ceremony and we all drove out to the stunning wedding venue of *Palacio Del Negralejo*, an 18th century palace with stunning scenic gardens, and courtyards. We celebrated their nuptials with a delicious wedding reception and then I had to rush off in order to be back at the show in time.

I celebrated my 21st birthday in Madrid whilst dancing at Scala. In the daytime I enjoyed a champagne seafood lunch on Gran Via. Fernando showered me with gifts and offered to host a drinks party for all the dancers at Joy Eslava, but instead I chose a beautiful intimate dinner at one of Madrid's most famous restaurants 'El Botin' and we invited Catarina and Miguel. My family sent cards and roses and Rosie gave me beautiful Spanish porcelain Lladro ballerina that I still treasure.

There seemed to be a birthday every week backstage in the dressing rooms. We would all contribute money to a collection and a gift was given to the birthday recipient in-between the first and second show. The birthday person would bring in cakes, crisps and other nibbles for everyone to enjoy.

Every few weeks I would book a few days off from the show to be with Fernando, we had 'swing' dancers in this big show which was amazing and it meant we could get them to take our place in the show, we basically paid them our nights wages we all loved the freedom that it allowed us. Fernando would fly me to Barcelona or Lanzarote so that we could be together and this was definitely still the 'honeymoon period' in our relationship.

I loved jetting off to Barcelona for the weekend and he had rented an apartment in Sitges, it was exciting seeing the sailing boat being built and coming to life week by week.

On the exterior of the yacht was a beautiful design that he had commissioned Cesar Manrique to design, a famous Spanish artist, many people commented on it when we were sailing.

One of these trips while I was in Lanzarote we were having such a lovely few days that neither of us wanted me to fly back to Madrid. Fernando suggested that I phone in and tell them I could not return yet because I had a bad ear infection and had been advised by a doctor that it was dangerous for me to fly. I did this and can you believe that the following morning I woke up in excruciating pain with an actual ear infection. I did go to the doctor straight away and he confirmed that I did have a bad ear infecton and couldn't fly, but the remainder of my days were awful since I really was dizzy and in pain with completely blocked ears. Karma!

Once back in Madrid, big brother Adey came over to visit, and during the time he was visiting the whole show suddenly had to be closed for a night. This was unheard of, but apparently there was some emergency mechanical work that needed to be done on the hydraulic stage.

We were beyond excited having the opportunity to have a big night out all together, what should we do we pondered over cigarettes and coffee.

A large group of us that were close friends all decided to go for dinner at a fabulous Mexican restaurant and then go on for drinks and probably end up in our favourite club, Joy Eslava. It must have been late November or early December by now because as we walked through 'Plaza Mayor' towards the restaurant, there was a huge beautiful Christmas tree that we all gathered around for a happy group photo. Dinner was delicious and fun, it's impossible to have a group of show performers around a table without someone starting some sort of impromptu performance. After dinner, since it was still too early to go to Joy Eslava, we decided to go and find a bar for drinks, as we wondered through the streets we stumbled upon a sex show! We unanimously decided, after far too much wine at the time, that it would be a great idea to go and see this show. The place was practically empty. I bet they couldn't believe their luck when around 20 of us all walked in, we managed to negotiate a deal on the ticket price explaining that we were the dancers from the Scala Madrid show. Within show business it is the code of conduct usually, that everyone offers discounted tickets to other performers. The show started and there were real live couples coming on to the stage having real live sex in front of our very eyes. I think we were all a bit shocked and laughed and giggled nervously. Thank goodness we had been drinking lots of wine beforehand.

We actually left early and headed off to make the most of our only ever night off, all together. We probably fell into bed around 5 a.m. No one seemed to get hangovers; I guess our liver enzymes were more efficient even though they were overused!

Aside from dancing at Scala, I had registered straight away with a couple of modeling agencies and sometimes picked up extra work. My thick curly hair came in useful for a Shampoo campaign and I was chosen to appear in their advertisements in glossy magazines and also the campaign was adorning the walls in the metro stations.

Fernando would fly into Madrid often. When he was in Madrid, we would go out with the others from the show, but I had noticed that he was starting to seem jealous of my fantastic life in Madrid.

One night in the shower, I noticed a hard lump in my lower ankle. I felt around and to my horror realised that it was the bullet, it was in fact still in my leg. I organized an x-ray and sure enough I was right.

I did not want to have it removed in Spain, so I organized that I would go back to the UK to do this and see my family at the same time. I did a flying visit back and Mum organized a belated 21st birthday party for me at home as a surprise and it was great to catch up with a few old friends.

I was whipped in and out of hospital where they removed the bullet and presented it to me in a little glass bottle and wrote on it Happy 21st. "Its not often we get to operate on a showgirl with a bullet in her leg!" the doctors said.

A few weeks later, Fernando needed to go back to Lanzarote and wanted me to meet him there.

One day, he was out at his office and I was mooching around in the villa. I found some packets of photos in the lounge, when I looked at them I noticed that the date was when I had been in the UK having my bullet removed. The photos were of him and a couple of his friends, at some sort of pool party, surrounded by girls draped all over him, sitting on his knee in bikinis. I was shocked and deeply upset and unsure what to do. I knew that in the past he had been a playboy, but I believed that now that he had met me, things were different.

Don't jump to conclusions I (foolishly) told myself. Anyway, we were about to sail around the world together and I comforted myself with that thought and chose to forget about the photos.

Back In Madrid there was great excitement because the choreographers and bosses from the big shows in Sun City, South Africa were coming to hold auditions in Madrid. There were several dancers who were coming to the end of their contracts who were interested in auditioning and they invited us all to audition for future contracts. I knew that I was going to leave soon and go sailing, but still wanted to attend the audition. Auditions were like taking a free dance class anyway, so there was nothing to lose for any of us. The minimum height requirement for the main show was 5'10" but they had another show called "Heavenly Bodies" which I was told was more Crazy Horse style and the height requirement was much shorter. Rosie and a handful of other successful dancers were offered contracts and once they finished in Madrid they headed to South Africa to join the Sun City show. They then spoke to me and said that if I was interested in joining the "Heavenly Bodies" show in Sun City after my contract ended to contact them. I was secretly ecstatic, even though I knew I would not be accepting. It was quite a while now since I had needed to attend an audition and it was great to feel that you had been successful and chosen again.

The sailing boat was almost ready and therefore it was time for me to give in my notice so that I could prepare to leave and join Fernando sailing around the world.

I was truly sad to leave the show in Madrid, I felt very emotional on my last night, and I put everything I had into my final two performances that night. When the final curtain fell, I was crying knowing how much I was going to miss these amazing friends and my Scala Madrid show family.

I sat down for the last time at my place in the dressing room in front of the mirror and started to pack away my make up and take down my photos that had been lovingly stuck up around my mirror of my family and Fernando.

There was a genuine outpouring of love and affection for me from me from my closest show friends and a collection had been organized to give me a watch as a leaving present. My friend Philip surprised me by giving me an enormous fluffy white poodle. It was so big I could not fit it in my suitcase and ended up carrying it in my hands the entire journey home to UK. Luckily there were fewer restrictions on luggage and big white poodles were allowed to be carried in hand luggage. The plane was not too busy so my poodle sat beside me and had his own seat much to the amusement of others.

I went back to the UK for Christmas arriving around the 23rd December. My flight was diverted and I ended up in Luton, Dad came to collect me, which was a nice and unexpected surprise and far better than trying to find a National Express coach.

I missed Madrid, the show and all my friends so much. I couldn't even speak to Fernando who was currently crossing the Atlantic Ocean with his crew, three of them in total. None of them were really experienced sailors so I was worried for them.

On December 30th I finally received a call from him telling me they were now safely in Isla De Margarita, a small Island just off Venezuela and this was where they would be spending New Years eve before sailing on to meet me in Martinique.

Mum, Ade and I walked around the corner to our local pub, The Potters Bar and spent a fun night there seeing in the new year with a few of Adeys old school friends. Dad stayed at home, he always went to bed on New Years Eve early and treated it just like any other night. Chalky was small and asleep in bed.

CHAPTER NINE

Sailing the Caribbean

Since this book is primarily about my dancing career, although it was undoubtedly an amazing experience to sail around the Caribbean on a sailing yacht for several months together, I'm not going to go into enormous detail but will give an insight before moving on to my next dancing contract.

A day or two later, Fernando had booked my flights and I flew out to join him, meeting him in the Caribbean Island of Martinique. My luggage was lost, but fortunately it arrived the following morning.

Everyone knows how beautiful the Caribbean Islands are. We also saw a lot of poverty though in these beautiful Islands and as a result felt at risk from crimes. We heard many harrowing stories from others sailing and they warned us to be very careful. There were definitely pirates operating in the area who would regularly ransack boats, taking passports, wallets, jewellery, electronics, clothes and anything else they wanted. We had to be careful about securing our dinghy and outboard too. As a result Fernando decided that I should learn to use the handgun that he had on board in case of emergencies. Fortunately I never had to put it to use and I don't think it would have been a good idea to resist armed attackers, better to just let them take what they want. All of those things can be replaced, lives cant.

Rojo and Azul the two parrots had crossed the Atlantic and were here on board with us, so it was lovely having them here too, a little taste of home. We met a couple who had a tiny pet monkey with them on board their yacht and due to an emergency they had to head immediately back to the USA and asked if we would take the monkey, which we did. The monkey was so cute, he was tiny and we called him Tarzan. Monkeys, even tiny ones like Tarzan are high maintenance though and in my opinion should not be kept as pets no matter how cute they are. Tarzan became sick and we spent a lot of money at the vets trying to get him better, but sadly he did not survive.

Fernando spent a lot of time complaining about all of the Islands that we visited, saying that they weren't what he had expected.

Our expectations versus the reality are often hugely different in life.

Stuck together on board a small sixty foot sailing yacht, the longer I spent alone with Fernando, the more I realised how much I missed dancing and my friends.

After a few months, due to the economy taking a turn for the worse Fernando suddenly had some huge problems back in the Canary Islands with his businesses and we were forced to abandon our sailing. I was secretly excited to be leaving the boat and couldn't wait to see some of my friends and family.

There was quite a lot to organise before we could fly back to Spain. Azul and Rojo were being transported back separately to Lanzarote at great expense via Madrid. A professional delivery crew would deliver the sailing boat back to Lanzarote.

Back in Lanzarote, it was very stressful. We were growing apart rapidly and he was becoming quite disrespectful the way that he spoke to me. Feeling desperately sad and lonely I booked a flight to go home for a visit.

A couple of nights before I was due to fly home to UK we were out in one of his clubs and he disappeared for a long time, eventually I decided to go to his office and see if he was there, as I walked in deliberately quietly, I heard his conversation on the phone. He was arranging for a girl that he had met in Venezuela over New Year and obviously been unfaithful to me with, to come over and stay with him while I was going to be in the UK.

I had heard everything and felt sick and heartbroken.

The conversations we had that night and the following day were pretty pointless. Basically he admitted that he had invited the girl from Venezuela over to stay with him. He talked about the three of us all living together as one happy family when I returned! He had delusions of being Hugh Hefner and having several girlfriends all living together with him at the same time, but I made it very clear to him that if she came then I would not return. He honestly didn't seem bothered that his unfaithful behavior was now causing an end to our relationship and he wasn't.

When he drove me to the airport, I cried the whole way. I felt completely heartbroken inside knowing that this was the end of our relationship. I also cried the whole plane journey home and the other passengers must have wondered what on earth was wrong with me.

I spent a very sad couple of months in the UK and decided it was time to get myself back to dancing. I started to look around for work and sent my CV off to a few people. Within a few days I was called by Jose Montes, a very well known and highly respected Spanish Choreographer and producer who had lots of big shows all around the world, in places like South Korea, Portugal, Malaga and Tenerife. Jose offered me a contract, which I accepted in his High Society ballet in Tenerife, the largest of the Spanish Canary Islands and ironically a neighbouring Island to Lanzarote.

CHAPTER TEN

Tenerife

MY ADDRESS

Hotel Martina, apt 507B, Avenida de Colon, Puerto De La Cruz

So here I was ironically back in the Canary Islands, but this time in the Island of Tenerife where I had never been to before.

I arrived late at night and took a taxi from the airport as instructed up to the north of the Island to Puerto De La Cruz. I remember nearing the North of the Island and driving through a long tunnel next to the sea, the driver told me that we were nearly there. This winding coast road reminded me a little of the road from Nice to Monaco. I checked in to Hotel Martina and unpacked my case ready to start rehearsals the following day. I opened my bedroom window to smoke a cigarette outside of it and breathed in the warm evening air mixed with the smell of tobacco. I could hear South American type music playing called *meringue* music and see and hear people laughing and chatting below a few floors down in the Hotel bar and terrace area. I felt happy to be back in the Canary Islands, I loved the climate here.

The following morning I headed to the Lago Martianez to meet Paul the Dance Captain who was British and started rehearsals. Paul told me that the whole show was changing soon and a new Spanish Ballet and new acts would be coming for the new production, which we would be rehearsing during the daytime whilst performing the existing show at night. This was set to be a grueling period.

After my first day of rehearsals I headed to the Lago Martianez in the evening to watch the full show and meet the rest of the cast.

Lago Martianez, or 'El Lago' as it was called, is an open air swimming pool complex in Puerto De La Cruz including several Islands, gardens, restaurants, bars and terraces. Our showroom was located inside the complex, under the ground beneath the large lido of swimming pools. Once inside it was a huge shiny glittery showroom, very glitzy with black velvet seating, and the entire ceiling was decorated in small mirror mosaics, like a huge mirror-ball ceiling.

Jose Montes the boss, was standing at the bar and introduced me to Nello who was the singer in the show and the company manager in Tenerife, they were old friends.

Jose invited me to sit with him to watch the show. He had been an outstanding and celebrated dancer himself when he was younger and was a lovely man who chatted to me in fluent English. I loved the show and choreography, it was slick and polished and the costumes were very elaborate.

For the first few days, I went back to the Hotel and cried every night. I was feeling the strain of the last few months breaking up with Fernando and it brought it all back to me being back in the Canary Islands, I felt as though I could see him in the nearby Island if I looked hard enough out to sea. I felt sad and lonely at the new show, they all seemed to have their own lives already.

I did three days of rehearsals including a dress rehearsal and then was thrown into the show. I remember feeling nervous but pleased to be in the show already.

The show was full every single night with tourists, mostly Europeans and the majority Italians who seemed to dominate this northern area of Tenerife.

A few days later the new Spanish Ballet arrived and came in to meet the cast and introduce themselves.

Imagine my absolute surprise and delight when it turned out to be MY Spanish ballet that I had been working with the year before in Scala Madrid. My dear friends, Rosa, Vicente and Miguel and others. I was *so* happy. Suddenly I had my old friends here and they were really excited and happy to see me too. I instantly started hanging out with them socially after the shows and going to flamenco bars and gay clubs with them, there were a lot of gay clubs in the north of Tenerife it was very much the gay capital of the Canary Islands.

A few girls were leaving the show, so there were a few new ones arriving. One of these new girls turned out to be Debbie, a stunning nude dancer that had also been in the Scala Madrid show with us. Debs and I had not known each other that well in Madrid because it was such a big show and she was in a different dressing room to me, but we knew each other well enough to be happy and excited to be working together again and we were both grateful to have a familiar face and became great friends. Suddenly, Tenerife was starting to feel comfortable and homely with all these familiar friends and some new ones too.

Life was relaxed and fun in Puerto De La Cruz, it was a holiday resort so completely full of tourists and happy holidaymakers. When we woke up around lunchtime we would wander down to the Lago and spend our afternoons sunbathing around the swimming pool, topping up our deep suntans whilst chatting, reading books and smoking. We never cooked and ate out at restaurants all the time, our life was just like being permanently on holiday.

Walking to and from our apartments we would pass by lots of photograph shops, remember then digital cameras were not yet the norm, so everyone bought films to load in their cameras, which then had to be taken into a photo shop to be developed and printed. As we walked past the shops we would always see ourselves in lots and lots of photos which were being printed in the shop windows, our show was a big attraction in this resort and practically every holiday maker booked to see it on one of their nights. Occasionally we would be recognised by some of the holiday makers sitting on the next table to us in restaurants who had seen the show, although to be honest we never knew how really because we all looked so different in the daytime without our show make up and costumes on.

There was always some drama going on backstage as is normal in showbusiness. A dancer called Sonia who I had just become friendly with did a 'bunk' from the show. Nello accused me of knowing and then later had to apologize when the concierge at the Hotel where I lived told him that Sonia had left a huge bag of toiletries for me in the reception. This then made Nello think that if she had confided in me, she would have just given the toiletries to me before hand.

Another sweet Welsh dancer called Sharon joined soon after me; we affectionately nicknamed her Blodwyn due to her adorable Welsh accent.

Paul, the dance captain and some of the other dancers rented studio apartments in the Hotel Martina that were privately owned by local landlords and they told us that there were others available. Sharon and me both rented a studio too and she lived in a studio directly beneath me. For fun I bought a bouncy ball and some long rope, then I put the bouncy ball in a carrier bag and attached the bag to the string and dangled it down from my window to bang on her window. The next day she said, "What the heck were we drinking last night? Because I could swear I heard someone knocking on my window." Sadly, Blodwyn was asked to leave the show after a very short period. The management had decided that she was too short and too heavy compared to the rest of the dancers. I sympathized greatly with her, remembering my own experience in Monaco, it could be quite a brutal business.

These days my weight was well and truly under control, I was obsessed with weighing myself and used to go into all of the pharmacies and pay a few *Pesetas*, the Spanish currency at the time, to go on the digital scales which gave you a printout of your weight. I kept them all in a drawer. I was very thin, still living off the dancer's diet of cigarettes, coffee and very little food, with 'the heartbreak diet' thrown in this time, the best diet remedy of all time, unfortunately.

One of my other new friends who also lived at Hotel Martina was a gorgeous male dancer called Jerko, from Belgium. Jerko was very charismatic and oozed positivity warmth and goodness as some people naturally do, he also had the looks of a film star and we became very close friends. He would confide in me all of his feelings about his dates, I would tell him all of my innermost feelings too.

One day, I remember standing with my back to Jerko looking out of his window and I was thinking very negative thoughts and without even seeing my face he felt it, he *knew*. We were so in tune with each other. With my back to him he shouted across the room to me, "What are you thinking? STOP it! I can feel negative thoughts and emotions coming from you." He was right. I could never tell him what I was thinking, but he was spot on.

Another new friend was a beautiful and bright dancer called Bee. Bee was always destined for a bright future whatever path she chose, for now she was dancing but later she re trained and became a successful journalist working for the BBC and a published author too.

Each and every dancer has to re invent themselves at some stage in their lives. Dancing professionally is a relatively short career like most professional sports. Sometimes it is because we become tired of dancing and the lifestyle and other times it is due to injury or because our bodies can no longer keep up with the high physical demands.

The good news is that due to our dance training and careers, we are very well equipped to adapt to whatever life throws at us. The skills that we learned as dancers are very transferrable as life skills elsewhere. When I told my teachers at school that I wanted to be a dancer, they would advise me that very few people actually became professional dancers and to get a good education and go to university first to have something to fall back on.

The problem for dancers is that to continue with our 'A' levels for a further two years and then do a degree for a minimum of three that is a total of five years, which in dancers careers is almost half of your peak years.

I couldn't wait to start dancing professionally and chose to leave school as soon as I had completed my necessary education. I do not have any regrets, it was 100% the right decision for me. I had decided very clearly in my mind that I would reinvent myself as and when I needed to in the future.

The new Dutch choreographer Maya arrived and we started rehearsing every day whilst we were still performing two performances of the existing show at night, realistically getting to sleep no earlier than 3 a.m. once we had wound down. It was great to all be learning the new choreography from scratch together and I felt it put everyone on a level playing field, rather than when you join an existing show and are the newbie. It was a great leveler and I couldn't help but smile to myself when one of the dancers who had been in the show for ever and was notorious for being unhelpful and bitchy to new girls, was one of the slowest to pick up the new choreography.

It was exciting and challenging for us all to be pushed and stimulated with new choreography. It was also hard going for everyone though, physically and emotionally challenging. As the rehearsals went on and on, exhaustion was setting in and tempers were fraying, resulting in tears and tantrums. But, as always happens when opening night arrives, smiles are plastered on our faces and everything is always all right on the night.

Tenerife hosts the second largest carnival in the world next to Rio de Janeiro, which is surprising considering it is a relatively small Island. Partially for this reason the capital city of Santa Cruz de Tenerife is twinned with Rio de Janeiro. The Carnival occurs every year usually in early February and attracts people from all over the world and takes over the capital city. Carnival was just incredible. Everyone dresses up in elaborate fancy dress costumes and thousands of people dance and mingle on the streets, buying drinks from the 'chiringuitos' (stalls) until the early hours of the following day. Most of the men dress as ladies and there is a running race where they must wear heels no less than 10 cm in height. Jerko and I made our own matching costumes and dressed as sisters, we all got into the carnival spirit and it was the most amazing atmosphere to go out and have the whole town dancing in costumes. I have never seen or experienced anything like this anywhere else.

My contract was drawing to a close. Nello our boss made it very clear that he wanted me to renew and offered me more money to stay and made a big fuss regularly telling me that he would be very upset, if I even considered leaving, which was flattering.

But I was unsure. I was still honestly heartbroken inside the whole time that I was in Tenerife. I was always hoping that Fernando would turn up on my doorstep, which was not far away being a neighboring Island and beg forgiveness, but he never did. He knew which show I had joined through friends of mine in Lanzarote, so he could have easily found me if he had wanted to. The reality was, the Venezuelan girl had left and he was enjoying being *Mr. playboy* again I heard through the same friends.

Mum had sent me an article about the Island of Jersey and the shows. Dick Ray had a well-known cabaret there called Caesars Palace and also owned Jersey opera house, where during the heyday of tourism, the summer farces that he put on were huge sell outs, including famous names like John Inman, Les Dennis, Vicky Michelle, Lionel Blair and Barbara Windsor to name a few. He was a very well know British impresario. Show business was in his family and in his blood.

I decided to look into maybe doing a summer season in Jersey and sent off my CV and photos to Dick. I wanted to see my Grandmother Florence, 'Nanny Smith' who I had not seen now for around 7 years due to dancing around the world and the rest of my Jersey family. I thought it could be quite nice to do a completely different dancing contract somewhere that spoke English and I had always loved spending time in Jersey growing up with our family there.

So I was pleased when a letter arrived for me offering me a job as a dancer for the summer season at Caesars Palace Jersey, with a contract inside ready for me to sign and return.

I was undecided though and put the contract in the desk draw at my apartment.

Several weeks later I dug out the contract and wrote back to Dick Ray with my signed contract enclosed.

As I ran off stage following the final curtain on my last night, I felt the usual mixture of emotions. The cast all hugged me and as soon as I had removed my feathers for the last time, Jerko picked me up and dunked me In the shower! I knew I would miss them all so much but felt I needed to move on to pastures new.

LANZAROTE, PAELLA ON THE BEACH WITH DAWN

LANZAROTE WITH DAWN

SCALA MADRID, BACKSTAGE DRESSING ROOM

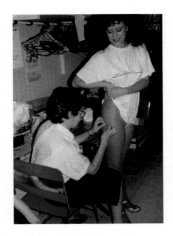

SCALA MADRID BACKSTAGE THE SASTRE QUICKLY FIXING MY FISHNET TIGHTS

SCALA MADRID FINALE FEATHERS

SCALA MADRID OPENING FEATHERS COSTUME

SCALA TOP HAT TAP ROUTINE

SCALA BACKSTAGE VIKING COSTUME

TENERIFE, ISLA DEL LAGO, GREEN & PINK FEATHERS

**TENERIFE, CLOSE UP SHOWGIRL MAKE-UP WITH
TOP & BOTTOM LASHES MAKING BIG, BEAUTIFUL EYES**

TENERIFE, ISLA DEL LAGO, SPANISH *GITANA* ROUTINE, (FAR LEFT)

TENERIFE WITH FRIEND & RENOWNED SPANISH DANCER VICENTE RENERO

TENERIFE LAST NIGHT SHOWER DUNKING WITH JERKO

CHAPTER ELEVEN

Jersey

MY ADDRESS

Caesars Palace Jersey, Flat 1, Greve De Lecq, St Ouen, Jersey

After a brief spell back at home seeing my family, my suitcase was all packed again and I headed off to Birmingham airport to fly to Jersey. Dad drove me to Birmingham airport. For once Dad even seemed excited about my dancing contract since it was in Jersey.

The beautiful Island of Jersey is the largest of the Channel Islands and is located just 14 miles off the French coast of Normandy. Jersey is one of the British Isles but is a self governing parliamentary, meaning it has its own banking and legal systems as well as its own courts of law.

This unique Island has a fascinating history for somewhere so small, only nine miles by five and a population of around 100,000 people. It offers so much and is a very special Island.

Soft golden sand beaches, rugged cliff walks, exotic flowers and palm trees due to the warmer climate, locally produced food, historic castles and ruins. The country lanes are dotted with honesty boxes where you can buy freshly picked produce and leave the right amount of money. It is a very safe and honest Island. It is also famous for its pretty brown cows and dairy produce, which is now exported worldwide.

The Channel Islands were the only part of the British Isles to be occupied by German forces between 1940 until May 9th 1945 when Jersey was liberated. My father and his family were all there during the occupation. Dad remembered very little but my Grandmother and other family and friends who were there during the occupation have told me their stories. They suffered incredible hardship.

I am writing this book during the Covid 19 lockdown in 2020 and we are all finding it a challenging time in our own way. I remind myself how hard it was for them during the occupation and feel grateful and privileged every day when I consider that during our global pandemic we have home comforts, we can read, work from home, educate our children on line, talk to our loved ones all around the world and keep in touch through social media. We have news, entertainment and most importantly, fridges and cupboards stocked with medicine and food. They had *none* of these things.

I was collected from the airport and taken straight down to Caesars Palace, which was situated at Greve De Lecq, on the beautiful and rugged north coast of Jersey. Greve De Lecq is in the Parish of St Ouen and has a beautiful golden sandy beach, sheltered from the wind by high cliffs.

Caesars Palace Jersey was situated here in the pretty bay and was an established and well-known cabaret venue for live shows and summer seasons where many famous faces had launched their careers.

I met one of the other dancers called Kim who had also just arrived and we were shown to our accommodation. Directly behind Caesars Palace there was staff accommodation for the dancers, singers and comedians, the manager and a few of the bar staff. I was sharing a room with Kim, while Jo and Claudia, two of the other dancers, shared the other bedroom in our apartment and we had our own little kitchen that we all shared and a bathroom. We were across the road from the sandy beach and there were three pubs and some beach cafes nearby, so we were happy.

The other female dancer in the team, Anya, a friendly Geordie girl lived on the Island with her family and some of the others lived in the capital town, St Helier at the other accommodation that Dick Ray owned at Jersey Opera House.

Rachel Ray was one of the first people that I met, a pretty blonde Jersey girl and Dick's daughter. She was the swing dancer and this was her first professional dancing job, she was 17 and it reminded me of myself being the same age on my first job in Spain. Not only was she an aspiring dancer she was a talented singer too.

Her glamorous Mum Peggy had been a professional singer and she had inherited her mums strong singing talent and amazing stage presence. Rachel was genuine and down to earth and I liked her instantly. Daniel was Dick and Peggy's son and our Stage Manager and Sound Technician, he was bright and witty. Both Rachel and Daniel had an amazing sense of humour; it obviously ran in the family. I warmed to them both instantly and knew we would be great friends.

On the first day of rehearsals, we went inside the showroom to warm up. I remember that I was shocked how small the venue was and the stage, a simple rectangular shape stage, no multi level stages here. Obviously I had been dancing in completely different venues around Europe in much larger companies on a totally different scale and there was no way you could compare, it was a completely different offering. Our stage alone in Madrid was bigger than the entire stage and auditorium of Caesars Palace together.

The format of the show was a couple of comedians, a hugely popular and talented singer, called Stuart Gillies, us dancers and the Roger Bara band. The acts and choreography were great. I quickly realised that when the curtain opened in this show, it was going to be down to us and our dancing skills to fulfill the audience, there were no fountains, ice rinks or Viking ships.

Most of our costumes were quite old with hundreds of names in them crossed out from previous dancers, but we had a wonderful wardrobe mistress, Susan, who worked her magic with the costumes and the budget that she had available to her. Underneath the stage lights the costumes sparkled and looked fabulous, fulfilling the audiences' expectations, which was all that mattered.

Caesars Palace was a fun place to work with coach loads of tourists arriving 6 nights a week to see the show.

This was a typical seaside summer season variety show and a visit to see a summer show was still a big tradition in British seaside holiday destinations.

On Sundays, since Dick owned Jersey Opera House, we were to appear in another show for part of the season, called the Black and White Minstrel Show and we were paid extra for this. Nowadays these types of shows have been banned due to the offence it caused by white performers blacking-up their faces for the performance in a variety type show, which consisted of traditional minstrel and country songs as well as show tunes, and music hall numbers with lavish costumes.

The first routine we learned was a music hall song called "Boiled beef and carrots," followed by another well-known cockney type song "Knees up Mother Brown."

Rachel had started to date Tony, a fun-loving guy from Durham originally and we all became close friends and still are. According to Tony, my face had been a *picture* when I was being shown the choreography and hearing the music for the first time.

I guess galloping around singing about boiled beef and carrots was just so different from the glamorous shows that I was used to performing in. Truth is told, once I got over the initial shock, I actually did really enjoy it. Plus, I have always been a versatile dancer and it was fun to do different choreography. Also, in the big European shows, as well as being beautiful showgirls in feathers we always had to do several other really fast paced routines and exhausting French cancans, tap routines, modern jazz routines all styles of choreography.

It was our dear friend Tony who nicknamed me 'ISG' which was his code for *international showgirl*. I guess because I had arrived in Jersey fresh from finishing my contract in Tenerife, being a *'fabulous'* showgirl and all the other big European shows that I had appeared in by now.

I loved the nickname and accepted it with pride.

At the start of each summer season there would be a 'Variety' welcome lunch held at the Grand Hotel on the Esplanade in St. Helier. Everyone dressed to impress at this lunch and it was a chance to meet all of the other show business performers who were here for the summer season and check out the 'competition' from the other shows. Throughout the course of summer, all of the shows on the Island would do charity collections after our shows to raise funds for the Variety club charity, which helped needy children all around the world.

Each week we had Monday club lunches, where acts and entertainers from all of the shows on the Island were invited to gather for lunch, hosted by a different Hotel each week and the money we paid for the lunch, went to the variety club charity. It was a great way to get to know other entertainers on the Island and find out the news and gossip from the other shows. During the Monday club lunches, any performers who wanted to would get up and entertain with a song, short set of music, magic, or short comedy routine. The other acts would all cheer and clap while secretly whispering behind their hands to one another: "He's not as funny as our comedian." "She can't carry a note in a bucket." "Didn't know Les Dawson was on keyboards today." But it was all good fun and raised a lot of money.

Jersey was turning out be a fun summer season for me. Often, at night after the show, Rachel and I would end up in Peggy's kitchen smoking Peggy's elegant looking *Du Maurier* cigarettes, which came in a beautiful red box. We would end up singing songs like "Sisters, sisters never were there such devoted sisters" and "We're just two little girls from Little Rock." Rachel and I had ideas of us being a singing double act at one point, but I am not a singer, I can sing in tune and belt out a song in the chorus enough to get me through an audition, but it was always my dancing skills carrying me.

I was earning the least money that I had ever been paid in this show, but at least our accommodation was included.

To earn extra money, in the daytime I had contacted a couple of local agencies and started to be offered modeling and promotion work. This could be anything from photo-shoots for magazines or newspapers promoting products such as Jewellery, or computer games, fashion shows, or standing in stores promoting new fragrances or cars or alcohol that had launched. These jobs were usually good fun and the extra money usually swiftly spent on fabulous new shoes or clothes.

I decided as soon as I arrived in Jersey that this was now a great opportunity for me to learn to drive, after leaving the UK aged 17, I had never wanted to try to learn to drive in other countries in a different language, so now was my chance. Jo and I enrolled in driving lessons with the same driving instructor and each week did our lessons. Claudia, one of the other dancers had brought her car over with her for the summer and she was so kind, helping us with extra tuition. Claudia was a beautiful person in every way and she loved to attend church on Sundays.

I also enjoy going to church services. I find it peaceful and am grateful for an opportunity to reflect and be thankful. I have never felt though that I must go to a church to pray and thank God, I do this anywhere I choose.

It was fantastic to be back in Jersey where I had spent so much time as a child and see my Grandmother, "Nanny Smith." I enjoyed catching up with all of my relatives again. My cousin Dominic who Is great fun had recently returned to the Island from working around the world on cruise ships, so myself and the dancers had great fun socializing with him and his friends down at the Gun site beach. Mum, Dad and Chalky came over for two weeks and Dad had the genius idea to buy a cheap secondhand car rather than rent one, and then at the end of the two weeks he would give it to me. This was amazing! as soon as I passed my test, I had my own little silver Mini Metro to drive around in.

Dad may not have been as supportive as I wish he could have been to me as a father in some ways, but I realise now that he was a product of his time and family. He grew up in a large family under difficult circumstances, with a controlling and physically abusive father.

Dad also had many good points too that I am eternally grateful for. He taught me to appreciate things, from the food on the table to my dancing lessons, he made me see the value in everything that he and Mum worked so hard to provide for us and he was *extremely* hard working. He was not a drinker or a gambler or a womanizer. He did *his* best; with the very limited emotional awareness he had learned from his parents.

Every summer in Jersey there is the most wonderful carnival called the 'Jersey Battle of Flowers', which started in 1902. This is one of the most impressive floral carnivals in the world. There are spectacular floats that are works of art decorated in thousands of fresh flowers. There are beauty queens and celebrities, musicians, dancers, majorettes and entertainers all parading along the beach front in St. Helier. Creating a wonderful atmosphere. In the weeks leading up to battle day, there are barns and warehouses all around the Island with locals working through the night finishing these masterpieces, all hoping to take the coveted major prize of 'Prix d'Honneur'. Caesars Palace hired a vintage open topped vehicle for us to take part in the parade and we all dressed up in costumes from the show, advertising our show and throwing confetti into the crowds. It really is a wonderful event to take part in and this was one of the highlights of the summer season. I remembered taking part in the Battle Of Flowers as a child too with my cousin Donna and the Brownie Guides club marching along the Esplanade dressed up as chocolates.

About two months before the end of the contract, I went into a designer menswear shop in St Helier called *Chex* to look for a birthday present. I was with Jo. As I paid for the shirt and got chatting to the manager, he asked if I would be interested in a Saturday job. I couldn't believe it, I accepted happily. I loved having regular extra money and also got a hefty staff discount if I wanted to buy anything, even though it was menswear, the girls and me bought the jeans and T-shirts. The owner, Jonny was a really nice guy and became a genuine friend. My son Danny did his first ever Saturday job at Chex too, with history repeating itself.

Towards the very end of the season Jo and I both had our driving tests scheduled in. Jo was first a week or so ahead of me. She went off in her white Caesars Palace T-shirt and some black shorts and came back grinning from ear to ear, she had passed first time. I was so pleased for her, she said that the instructor had noticed her T-shirt and asked if she worked there and she told him that she was a dancer at Caesars Palace. A week later when it was my turn, I decided to wear the same T-shirt for good luck and guess what, I passed first time too.

Passing my driving test is one of those vivid memories of my life. The thrill of having that independence is something you cannot explain. I remember running to a phone box in the Royal Yacht Hotel to excitedly phone my Mum and tell her the good news.

I spent my last few weeks in Jersey driving around the beautiful Island as much as possible. I never got bored driving around the leafy lanes, passing beautiful Lavender fields, golden beaches, and pretty brown Jersey cows.

Then something that I *never* expected happened. Towards the very end of the season, Fernando called me and was in London and wanted to come and see me. He said that he had already booked flights to Jersey and a room. I forced myself to be strong and made a last-minute phone call and told him not to come, even though I was aching to see him.

There was too much water under the bridge now.

It felt good to choose to walk away from him.

CHAPTER TWELVE
Switzerland

MY ADDRESS

Hauptsrasse 62, Degersheim, CH9113

My good friends Nikki 'Pickle' and Vicky from Scala Madrid were both dancing together on a contract in Switzerland and Pickle told me that there was a vacancy coming up. This fitted in perfectly with the end of my contract in Jersey so I wrote off and sent my photos through along with my C.V. and was so excited to be offered the job.

After a quick stop off back in England seeing the family, I flew into Zurich and took a taxi for just under an hour to the St. Gallen region in Eastern Switzerland, to a small village called Degersheim where *Retonios Magic Casino* show was to be found.

Degersheim was like something from a picture book, with beautiful snowy mountains full of pine trees and traditional looking chalet type homes.

The Magic Casino was Switzerland's answer to Las Vegas and was nicknamed *'Las Degas'*.

Retonio Breitenmoser the owner at that time was a magician and ventriloquist who had performed in Las Vegas at The Flamingo Hotel on the strip for many years, (I also had my *hen party* lunch here). He returned to his home, Switzerland and opened The Magic Casino. I never quite understood how this large cabaret show ended up in this picturesque village, but the audiences would come by the coach load night after night and fill the venue. As the guests entered the large elaborate auditorium they were wowed with a magnificent Taj Mahal 101 key Mortier organ. Our dinner show offered a unique and spectacular combination of Magic, comedy, songs and exotic costumes and dancers along with pyrotechnical fireworks. We were not only dancing in this show, we would be magically levitated, changed or disappear into thin air in the land of illusion. There was no gambling here.

The choreography in this show was probably my least favourite ever though; it wasn't creative and just didn't flow. The choreographer seemed to have tried to cram in as many movements as she possibly could into the shortest space of music. It looked awkward when the dancers were going from one move to another without having time to execute the movements elegantly, correctly and to the full range.

Also for one routine we were dancing in very high-heeled red stiletto boots that were not dancers shoes. Dancing in heels restricts choreography anyway and these silly boots were just bought from a regular shoe shop, they would have been fine for a night out tottering from the bar to a table for dinner but definitely not for fast paced choreography to try and dance triple pirouettes in.

Degersheim

We only had around four performances a week, so we had lots and lots of free time to enjoy the snow and beauty of Degersheim

I absolutely loved my time in this pretty small village. The girl dancers all lived together and shared a big typical Swiss looking chalet house with quaint small paned windows outside, set over several floors, it looked like something from a *Heidi* story book. The boy dancers lived in a separate house around five minutes walk away.

It was winter so there was always snow outside and the entire village looked beautiful and dreamy. Since I was the last one in the house I had whichever bed was available and shared a room with a dancer called Adele for a few days and then when another dancer left, I moved up into the top floor bedroom in the attic of the house and had the room to myself.

No words will ever do justice to the magnificent and tranquil view I took in each morning as I opened my shutters to look out of the window. The sheer beauty of the sun sparkling on the fresh snow covered mountains, with hundreds of pine trees was simply breathtaking and I did my best to commit this view to memory, knowing that I was witnessing something very special.

We had so much childlike fun playing in the snow, walking in the snow up the mountains and rewarding ourselves with a delicious hot chocolate. Pickle, Vicky and myself would go up to the top of hills with old carrier bags and slide down using them as a make shift sledges. It was great exercise too.

The absolute highlight each week for us was the discovery of the most magical place called the Brockenhaus.

The Brockenhaus was an Aladdin's cave of secondhand clothes and treasures donated by wealthy Swiss residents for resale. We bought all sorts of clothes and trinkets. We would excitedly make our way up there around twice a week when it opened and find amazing bargains.

Our salary was quite meager and Switzerland was very expensive so we were careful with our money and shared food and dinners, our favourite being egg and chips washed down with pints of ribena. I even gave up smoking, which saved me a small fortune.

In the street where our house was, there were some young local boys who realised that ours was a house full of young ladies.

Early evening around dinnertime, they would often throw snowballs at the house window, or sometimes directly at us when we were coming out down the steps on our way to walk to the casino,

It was all good fun but we wanted to get our own back on them.

I decided that I would be prepared, so I went outside scooped up a load of snow and put it in the freezer in balls ready to throw at them on our way out to work. I didn't really think this through because obviously having put in the freezer it was now very hard and solid!

There was a toilet also next to the front door of the house and sometimes the naughty boys would see the light go on and throw a snowballs at the window while we were in there, making us jump.

Pickle went into the toilet and I decided I would pretend to be one of the naughty boys and throw my snowball at the window as a joke. I was laughing to myself as I ran outside and threw the frozen snowball expecting to hear a thud and her shriek, but my hard snowball actually smashed the window so I heard the shattering of glass and her shrieking *very* loudly, I felt awful. I ran back up inside, Pickle came out swearing, "Those bloody boys just broke the window throwing a snowball at me." I said, "No no, I'm so sorry it was me!" Once Pickle realized what had happened she saw the funny side of it. We made up an excuse to the bosses and said that the boys had broken the window so that I didn't get into trouble or have to pay for the window.

Christmas was almost here, so we all put our money together and bought a freshly cut Christmas tree for the house.

Switzerland was such a safe and honest place then, that all of the Christmas trees that were for sale were left outside of the supermarkets overnight and no one would have dreamed of stealing one. We looked around everywhere for fairy lights for the tree and weirdly there didn't seem to be any such thing, but what they did sell were little candleholders that clipped onto the branches of the Christmas tree and then you put real candles into them. We all remarked how dangerous it could possibly be and cause fires, but anyway since there was nothing else we did this. Obviously the real candles looked absolutely beautiful on the tree and we were very careful to not have any fires or accidents.

On Christmas Eve we walked to the nearby village church for the Midnight mass service. We felt as though we understood what was going on and recognized some of the hymns. As the service ended and the church bells rang out, we exited the church through the side door and fresh snowflakes were falling it was like something from a film, this was definitely one of my most magical Christmas memories ever.

The following day we all opened our presents around the tree and then got ready for Christmas lunch, which was to be at our girl's house. We were all allocated roles, mine was to help prepare the table and make drinks, which I did with great joy in my new cream coloured fluffy mule slippers that Aunty Jean had sent to me for Christmas. One of the male dancers, 'Canadian Mike' as we called him since there were two male dancers called Mike, had volunteered to cook the turkey and it was outstanding.

On New Year's Eve after the show, we all went to the boys' house and had a great party, drinking cocktails and eating delicious fondue style food dipping meats and bread into the delicious Swiss cheese.

A highlight of my contract in Switzerland was that my dear friend Jerko came to visit me. I was so overjoyed to see him again and we talked into the early hours of the morning catching up on each other's news. The Swiss contract came to an end and I had decided to go back to Jersey for a second summer season.

CHAPTER THIRTEEN
Jersey 2

MY ADDRESS

34 Seaton Place, St Helier, Jersey

As soon as I returned to jersey I started smoking again, afraid that I might gain weight if I did not. This year we were all going to be living in town rather than out at Greve De Lecq. Jo and I were sharing a flat in St Helier at Jersey opera house with Daniel and his girl-friend. Rachel and Tony shared a flat upstairs. We all lived at 34 Seaton Place and also there was an Australian actress Jess, who was starring in the Jersey Opera house show. We all became good friends and shared a memorable summer season with lots of laughs and a few highs and lows, but mostly highs. Whenever I have watched the series *Friends,* it reminds me in many ways of our close friendship group that year and fun times at 34 Seaton Place.

It was great being in the bustling capital of St. Helier with everything in walking distance.

Jo had returned for the season too and had exciting news, during her winter pantomime she had worked with a magician and comedian Martin

Daniels, the son of the Paul Daniels the world famous magician and they had fallen head over heels in love. Jo and Martin soon announced their engagement and Martin came over and rented a bungalow for him and Jo to live in on the beach, so although Jo and I were roommates, I basically had our room to myself that season. Jo asked me to be one of her brides-maids, which I was super excited about. Paul Daniels and his lovely wife Debbie Mc Gee came over to Jersey and we all celebrated their engagement.

This year we were all super excited because the star of the Sunday show at Jersey Opera House that we would be performing in was the celeb-rity dancer Wayne Sleep. After training at the Royal Ballet School and becoming a principal dancer with several of the best-known ballet com-panies, he then formed his own dance company called DASH, which per-formed, all around the world. It is well documented that he was a very close friend with the late Princess Diana and I could see why she enjoyed his company, he was full of fun and banter and he loved to party, a real show business character.

At the end of another lovely Jersey summer season, we were all sad to learn that this show was to be Dicks last one ever at Caesars Palace, tourist numbers were declining and the shows were really struggling.

Dick instead was going to do a touring show the following year, which I was offered a place in. I was unsure because I had experienced the touring show in Mallorca and not enjoyed the touring aspect. I accepted anyway.

Park Lane London – Grand Order of Water Rats Ball

Every November there is a grand Water Rats Ball in London where household names from all over the world come together to entertain, sup-port, and fundraise.

Dick Ray was a member of The Grand Order of Water Rats, which is a British show business charity. The charity raises money by organiz-ing shows, and other events to assist other members of the entertainment industry who due to illness or old age may be in need.

Dick and Peggy invited me to join their table along with Rachel, Tony, Daniel and a few others. This year it was at The Grosvenor House Hotel in Park Lane. We all dressed up in our black tie outfits. I have never seen so many celebrities in one room. I remember Brian May from the band Queen and a few other musicians getting up on stage and doing an impromptu performance. There were lots of famous British Actors and musicians and even Hollywood names too. It was an amazing night and a lovely way to say 'farewell' before we headed off for our respective winter contracts.

CHAPTER FOURTEEN

Japan

MY ADDRESS

Uedakan Hotel, Togura 3055, Hanisinagun, Nagano-ken, Japan

had been looking through *The Stage* towards the end of our summer season to see what auditions there were and decided to try for a winter season in Japan. I had sent in my CV to Vivas International, a well-known company and had been offered a 3-month contract as a dancer and Dance Captain, starting rehearsals soon after my summer season finished and the Water Rats Ball.

Rehearsals for Japan were quite unusual but fun too. Our bosses, Barry and Jackie were husband and wife and they had been doing Japan contracts for years and years.

I always saw them in The Stage and knew lots of other girls who had worked for them. They were also one of the only companies who offered contracts in Japan where you were not expected to do *hostess* work; this was not like the hostess work in Italy. Nearly all of my dancer friends who had worked in Japan had to do hostess work after the show, this basically meant that aside from being dancers in the show, in-between or following their performances they had to wear supplied evening gowns and pour clients drinks (the Japanese tend to buy bottles of whisky) light their cigarettes, chat to them and pretend to be interested in their conversations, oh and of course, sing Karaoke with them.

This did not appeal to me at all, even though everyone earned extremely good money on these contracts, at least double what we were paid in say, Paris or Spain. I still was not prepared to have to be a hostess, there was nothing sexual involved but I just thought how boring it must be and that was not what I had trained to do as a dedicated dancer.

So I found myself in the south of England near to Bognor Regis rehearsing for Japan. Jackie and Barry had two big caravans in the back of the garden and another Porta cabin, which they had turned into a dance studio. The dancers all lived in these caravans while we did our rehearsals, it was actually great because it meant we had no outgoing's and they would provide all of our meals for us and cook a healthy dinner for us all every night which meant we ate well. It also meant for them that if there were any girls that they thought should lose a pound or two, they could help by offering only healthy food choices.

Every night we would all sit around the huge table in their kitchen, about 12 of us and have dinner together which was actually very nice, we felt like one big, slightly crazy, family.

During the daytime we did our rehearsals in the Porta cabin it, was winter now so it was absolutely freezing in the caravans and the Porta cabin studio, so we made sure we warmed up particularly well before starting to dance. The worst thing was the shower facilities that they had built outside in a sort of wooden garden chalet, it would have been OK in the summer, but the water was not hot at all, barely tepid. It was quite painful, but at least it meant we all got in and out the shower as quickly as possible.

Our favourite thing about rehearsals was the pub. Each evening after dinner we would walk around 3 minutes down a short little track from their Bungalow and at the bottom was a cute pub directly next to a railway line.

After two weeks of rehearsals, we were all ready to go to Japan and Barry drove us to Heathrow airport with all our costumes and trunks and off we went with a smile, a wave and a commercial sized tub of Marmite. Thank goodness I did take the Marmite, because I did not like the Japanese food much at all at the time, so ironic because now I adore Japanese food.

Hong Kong

After a 10-hour flight on Cathay Pacific from Heathrow, drinking Gin and Tonics and smoking, as we were still allowed to do then on board aircrafts, we landed at the world famous Kai Tak airport in Hong Kong. This was quite a thrilling and scary experience, the planes seemed to swoop in tightly between the residential skyscrapers, enabling us to see in through the windows of resident's homes and land next to the sea, it felt as though the plane might not be able to stop in time and end up in the sea. There were a couple of aircraft that did end up overrunning the runway, plunging into the harbor and the airport was finally closed in 1998 and moved to a new, safer location.

We were staying in Hong Kong for four days, where we needed to process our visas and get some paperwork done on route to Japan. This was actually great for us, having a short holiday in Hong Kong. We were met at the airport by an agent and taken to Kowloon, to a large Hotel, which was called The Kowloon Panda Hotel. We went to an office and did the required paperwork with the agent and then he said he would contact us in a couple of days when the visas were ready and to enjoy our time in Hong Kong.

This was one of the smallest shows that I ever performed in, there were only three of us in the show, myself, Stephanie and Jo, we were all British. The three of us shared a room in Hong Kong and all got along well.

Vivas had given us a generous allowance of spending money for this time to cover food, drinks and any taxis we needed to take. They had warned us that if we were taking any taxis then we must ask at the Hotel reception before we left, to write down our destinations in Chinese, since the taxi drivers mostly did not speak English.

Unfortunately we forgot to do this on our first night out, the taxi driver didn't understand us at all and got very angry and annoyed with us driving around and kicked us out of the car. We had no clue where we were. We walked around until we found a Hotel and then asked their receptionists to help us, which they did, and eventually we found our way back to our Hotel.

Hong Kong was like nowhere else I had ever been before, the hustle and the bustle, the shops, the lights, the food, the sounds, the noise, the smells. We were surprised that no one seemed to speak English in any of the shops or restaurants we went to. The menus were not written in English, only Chinese *hanzi* characters, so when they handed them to us we were none the wiser. We just used to randomly point to something, like a lucky dip and see what we ended up with. We also had to get used to the fact that that there were no knives and forks, only chopsticks. We even bought a phrase book and pointed to pictures of knives and forks, but they would laugh and shake their heads. We soon became very good with our chopsticks because we had no choice. The shops were cheap and we bought lots of Clinique make up and toiletries and a few clothes.

We decided to get up early one day and take the star ferry from Kowloon over to Hong Kong Island. The crossing only took around 10 minutes, but it was a magical experience, passing traditional wooden sailboats, called junk boats with their large striking red sails.

Once we arrived on Hong Kong Island, we took a tour around the Island on an open top double deck bus and then went on the steep peak tram up to Victoria Peak where there are far-reaching views of the city and its waterfront.

Recently, Tom and I stayed on Hong Kong Island at The Mandarin Oriental Hotel, enjoying afternoon tea in the Clipper bar, and classic Cocktails in the Captains Bar. I thought back fondly to my time on the way to Japan with the other dancers.

Our visas were soon processed and we were ready to travel onwards to Japan.

It was night time and dark when we arrived in Tokyo Narita airport, we were told by Jackie and Barry that the agent would be there to meet us, but guess what? No one was there!

I managed to buy a phone card with my first Japanese Yen money that Jackie and Barry had given us for travelling and phoned them, Barry said call back in half an hour and in the meantime he would try to find out where the agent was.

While we were waiting there at the airport itself, we were ushered by the airport staff and police into a really small-designated waiting area in the airport in a little section that we were all made to stay in. No one was allowed to wander around the airport at night randomly. It was immaculately clean without any litter anywhere and I noted that all the workers at the airport had white gloves on. After a few more calls, and no sign of an agent, Barry told us to take a taxi to the nearby ANA hotel and stay there for the night. We were now to be met the following morning by the agent lady.

Fortunately, everything went to plan the next day and the lady and a man picked us up in a minibus and drove us to where we were to be living and performing, Uedekan Riverside Hotel in the town of Togura Kamiyamada, situated In Nagano prefecture.

Japan is made up of 43 'prefectures,' which are basically like states. We drove for around 4 hours through several boring, industrial looking prefectures and some very picturesque and pretty ones until we arrived.

Togura Kamiyamada has been tempting visitors dating back to the 19th century. Nestled in a beautiful valley and Situated on the western bank of the Chikuma River, Togura Kamiyamada is an *onsen* town, which means it is a natural hot spring town.

In Japan, in order for a spring to be called an 'onsen,' it cannot just be hot water; it must be over 25°C and contains a certain level of sulfur and other minerals with skin smoothing alkalinity. The water always felt hot to us and it took us a while to get used to the water temperature.

Japan has a rich and vibrant onsen culture. This is not just a place to wash, it is a place to relax and it is an integral part of Japanese peoples lives and helps keep them mentally and physically healthy. Ladies and men bathe separately and everyone bathes completely naked. At first, we were hesitant and nervous in the ladies staff area bathing naked with our colleagues, but we soon got used to it.

As soon as the guests arrive in this small town, the first thing everyone does is change into their *Yukata* which is like a dressing gown or robe and then this is the clothing that they wear for the entire duration, both indoors and through the streets of the town.

We arrived at the hotel which looked very ugly from the outside, a large grey concrete building that didn't seem to fit in really with its surroundings. We were greeted with traditional bowing, by the showroom manager and his wife. How polite they seemed. How wrong we were.

We were shown to our dancers accommodation, which was sort of like a great big studio that had been split into two areas by wardrobes acting as a divider. There were three lots of bunk beds in the sleeping area and a TV and then around the other side was a table to sit and eat at or write letters, a bathroom, a small kitchen area and a washing machine. We all chose a bunk bed and unpacked.

Japanese Toilets

The most exciting find in the Hotel, were the toilets. These all singing, all dancing toilets were technological wonders. The lid opens automatically, they play music and they deodorize, sterilize and wash the exact area that you choose with warm water. They can massage and blow dry once you have finished and they automatically flush, but the standout feature has to be the heated seat. These various controls turned the usually boring act of going to the toilet into something interesting and something that was definitely worth allocating more time for.

We noticed very quickly that no one spoke English at all. We also did not speak any Japanese. I had danced in Europe In countries where I did not speak the language, however the alphabet is more or less the same, so if you start to see the words written down enough times on certain items regularly, you start to know what it must mean. So for example in the supermarket in Spain, I quickly learned that *mantequilla* was butter, *agua* was water, *pain* was bread and so on, you can roughly have a guess at how to pronounce the word and make some sort of noise to make yourself understood, but in Japan, because the alphabet is completely different, it's all made up of pretty little sticks and shapes and squares and boxes and there is no way that you have any idea at all how to start to read or pronounce something.

The other thing that we picked up on quickly was that the body language and gestures were also very different. We kept noticing that the Japanese staff in the hotel would often touch the middle of their noses with their index finger whilst trying to communicate to us, why do they keep touching their noses we wondered? After a few days we managed to pick up that when they were touching their noses, they were saying the word *watashi*. We looked it up in our Japanese to English dictionary and found that *watashi* means 'I' or 'me', we worked out that they point to their noses, just like English people point to ourselves in the chest when we say *I* or *me*, Japanese people probably think that we are weird poking ourselves in the chest.

It was the first time that I've ever actually really considered that body language and gestures can be so drastically different from country to country and have such different meanings too.

Manager taught us that shouting the word *DAMMY* at the top of your voice with your arms crossed over your chest in an X sign, means *NO* or *NOT ALLOWED*.

Which brings me on to our new boss in Japan who we called *manager* 'Manager' was a weird looking Japanese guy, he always wore grey suits and looked typically Japanese but with curly afro type hair. He introduced himself to us as Manager, we never did find out his actual name, since he spoke no English and we did not speak Japanese, but he made it clear to us that we should call him simply 'Manager'.

His wife was introduced to us as the *"Mamasan"* we thought this was her name but later found out that Mamasan means a woman in a position of authority usually in charge of a Geisha house, or a bar or nightclub. So our cabaret room basically included all of those.

It was definitely a bar, every night when we made our way to the showroom; we could smell warm sake wafting through the air. Indeed, the audience were so drunk by the time we came on stage that every night when the curtain opened and we came out in our green feather opening costumes dancing to "Don't Stop Me Now" by Queen, we would take bets and count how many drunk men were lying on the floor in front of the stage. The funny thing was, that at some point during the show they would just stand up and take their seat back at their table and carry on drinking again.

Before and after our cabaret, Mamasan would come out and sing a few traditional songs in Japanese. The audience seemed to enjoy her singing, it sounded very drab to us. Manager was in charge of the sound and lighting for our show and the karaoke following the show.

Karaoke as everyone knows hails from Japan. The Japanese are crazy about it and it's easy to find everywhere. What I loved about Karaoke in Japan, is that no one judges your singing skills and everyone gets up and has a go, no matter how good or bad they are at singing.

In one of our local Karaoke bars we would often see the local Buddhist monks belting out songs on the karaoke. It is my favourite place ever to partake in Karaoke.

On our opening night, the show went really well and it also happened to be Jos birthday, so after the show we were invited into the cabaret room for drinks and birthday 'cake-ee' as they pronounced it in Japan. Manager and Mamasan had organized birthday cake and *Sake* for us to drink; Japanese rice wine with a strong nutty taste, it was the first time any of us had tried it. A couple of Geishas joined us at the table too to help with the socialising. In Togura Kamiyamada, we would see plenty of Geisha girls who were dressed impeccably with their thick unnaturally white make up on their faces dressed in their beautiful traditional outfits. Their dark and shiny hair was always worn up and full of decorations, they would sit alongside the gentlemen guests at our show and chat to the guests and light their cigarettes and pour drinks for them.

Geishas are considered entertainers; they train from childhood in various traditional Japanese arts, mastering singing, playing the samisen, dancing and the art of witty conversation. Their mothers or grandmothers who were also geisha usually train them.

On the second night after our show, Manager gestured to us to go into the show room again, we were all a bit tired since we were still getting used to everything and shook our heads and said no thank you and then we discovered the first grumpy, angry face of manager, which we basically saw for the rest of the contract! He made it very clear through his gestures that we had no choice and MUST go into the room; OK we thought lets just go for a quick drink to keep them happy. When we went into the bar and sat down, manager started saying something to us which we obviously didn't understand, he kept on an on and then we sort of managed to work out that he was saying "cheek dancing, cheek dancing" what does he mean we wondered? "Cheek dancing" we were somewhat confused, it sounded dodgy, he just kept saying cheek dancing and pointing to the male guests and the dance floor. He was writing down on a piece of paper how much extra yen we would earn if we did "cheek dancing". We were paid very well in Japan already, so the extra Yen was not going to convince us to change our minds to dance with men in yukatas, so we shook our heads vigorously saying NO! NO! His face was starting to look red and angry now.

Eventually, feeling somewhat bewildered and pressurized by a shouting manager, Jo and me eventually did get up and dance with a short Japanese man each. I was furious inside; I didn't come here to dance with strange men in yukatas. We had come to work here as professionally trained dancers.

After one dance I said to Jo and Steph, *"right, come on we are going"* and we left, much to the annoyance of manager who was looking furious and shouting his favourite word *'DAMMY'* to us and crossing his arms in the X sign across his chest.

Directly after we got back to our rooms, we quickly changed our clothes and headed straight out to the phone box and since I was the dance captain, I called Barry.

He was furious with them and said, "You just tell them you are English dancers and you do not do cheek dancing." I told him that we had already said that and Barry told me that he would speak to their agent who the Hotel had booked us through. This was a brand new contract for Vivas, so there were a few things that needed to be sorted out.

After that we were not asked to do cheek dancing again but manager started to be extra rude and mean to us, its hard to explain how, since we were not able to speak to each other in a language that either understood, but his actions and body language were just mean, cross, shouty and rude.

At Uedakan Hotel, the guest rooms were very traditional Japanese style, with straw like *Tatami* flooring, and *Shoji* walls, which are like, thin translucent paper on a wooden frame and a Futon on the floor to sleep on.

The ladies *yukatas* were a pretty pale pink colour and the gents were a lime green colour. We could identify which Hotel or Ryokan people were staying at by the colour of their yukatas as they wandered through the town. It was a small town with only a few hotels so it was easy to know where the guests were from. There was only our Hotel and one other in the town that had a cabaret with professional dancers and showgirls, so the showrooms were popular with guests from all of the other hotels and smaller ryokans too.

In Japan everyone takes off their outdoor shoes as they enter a venue, so you wear socks and flip flop type slippers indoors and when you go out-doors, you leave these at the entrance of the Hotel or Ryokan and change to wooden outdoor ones called *geta* (like hard wooden flip flops)

Then if you enter a bar or karaoke place the same thing happens, you leave your *geta* at the door and change into indoor slippers that are provided.

At nighttime, neon lights gently illuminated several streets in the town's small bar district, I can't tell you how funny and weird it seemed at first to see hoards of mostly male tourists, strolling through the streets, drinking and singing in karaoke bars in their *yukatas.*

Each night when it was approaching Show Time, we would take one of the staff lifts down to the ground floor of the Hotel and head to the showroom area. As we stood in the lift with whichever of the other staff may happen to be in there, none of whom spoke English, they would look at us in awe, because we were so tall compared to them. Also, they were mesmerized by our blue eyes and naturally curly hair which both Jo and I had, they loved it and would touch our hair in the lift, they were so sweet. Remember, this was not Tokyo, where they would be more used to seeing blondes and curls, this was rural Japan, where the Tokyo office workers came to relax and bathe naked in onsen, drink too much sake and whisky and sing karaoke and be entertained by cabaret dancers and Geisha girls!

A lot of the shows in Japan actually advertised for blonde dancers because this was so different and appealing to the Japanese people, a few friends of mine quickly died their hair blonde before going to Japan auditions and secured jobs and loaded their suitcases up with blonde hair colour to take with them. Vivas did not have any hair colour requirements and anyway we wore lots of different colour wigs and beautiful feather headdresses so you could not really tell what colour our hair was, actually we were all dark brunettes.

One night the Hotel owners wife, Tomako, came to watch our show. It turned out that she was having English lessons and she had invited some of the English teachers from her school with her to see our show. The teachers were from England and Australia, we chatted to them after the show briefly and when they left, Stephanie exchanged numbers with of one of the boys, an English guy called Saul. Thank God for this moment, they became our lifeline.

Japanese people do not celebrate Christmas, since only around 1 percent of the Japanese population is Christian, however, they do use it as a time to spend time together and exchange gifts. So, the hotel shut down for a couple of days and by Christmas eve, the only people that were actually left inside the hotel were us three, since everyone else went home to their families. Everything in the Hotel was locked up and in darkness other than our own room. We couldn't even get out of the front door to go for a walk or to the supermarket. We also discovered that we were locked in the Hotel. No one had thought or bothered to organize a key for us. Manager probably *had* thought and done this deliberately.

On Christmas morning, we woke up and exchanged our little gifts that we had bought one another. I had also done a treasure hunt for Jo and Steph all around the huge Hotel. We might as well make the most of being locked up in a Hotel I decided. As the afternoon rolled around we were getting more and more annoyed that Manager had not bothered communicating anything to us and left us locked inside the Hotel.

Steph phoned the English teacher Saul and thankfully he answered and told us to all come over and join them, they were all together having a party. We needed to catch a train since they lived around 20 minutes away and he gave all of the details to Steph.

We decided that somehow we would find a way out of this hotel.

We walked around every floor and managed to open a fire emergency exit door and we were out. We weren't sure how we would get back in, because once the door closed we couldn't open it again, but right now we didn't care.

We had great fun with the teachers and when we returned, we remembered that there was a window that was sometimes slid open in the ground floor ladies staff Onsen. Otherwise, we would smash a window. It would serve manager right for leaving us there all alone.

Luck was on our side, the window downstairs was unlocked and we climbed in, directly into the hot onsen water, but we didn't care and still full of Christmas cheer and drinks thought it was hilarious wading our way through the hot water, this time with our clothes on!

One day, the three of us stumbled upon what looked like a secondhand bicycle shop. We went inside, and within 5 minutes, by waving money around and pointing, the three of us left with a bicycle each. Quite an achievement since we didn't speak Japanese. They cost around the equivalent of 20 pounds. This has to be the best 20 pounds I ever spent. For the rest of the contract we rode around on our bicycles everywhere, enjoying the mountain and river scenery along the way, past rice fields and apple orchards.

There was a great long, flat, straight road that seemed to lead to nowhere and while cycling on it alone, in the very middle of nowhere I came across a vending machine. There was something wonderful about buying a hot Chicken soup or hot sweet tea from the vending machine in the middle of nowhere and cycling onwards.

I always felt safe in Japan, whether on my bicycle or walking around the town late at night. It was such an honest place. One evening the three of us found the local alcohol shop. We went in to buy a bottle of Vodka and there was no one there serving. Then, a local person came in, they took their bottle and left the correct amount of yen on the counter and left, so we did the same. Every week.

Japanese Food

The Japanese food was not something that I enjoyed at this time, especially raw fish, which ironically I now love. I finally discovered that I liked ramen, which is basically wheat noodles served in a hot meat broth with various vegetables, such as shitake mushrooms, bean sprouts and green onions, topped with a narutomaki, or naruto for short, a pink swirly thing that looks like candy but is actually a little fish cake. This region of Japan is also famous for soba noodles, which were made from buckwheat and often served chilled with a dipping sauce.

One meal that I especially recall was in a remote mountain that the teachers had discovered. It was not a restaurant but someone's traditional home. We walked up the snow-covered mountain and the lady cooked a roast suckling pig over a fire pit in the middle of her lounge. It tasted delicious, it was so bizarre but so memorable.

On another occasion, one of the English teachers invited us to visit a local school where they taught English to young children. The children were so unbelievably cute and laughed and giggled excitedly as we entered the classroom, they were enjoying practicing their basic English saying "hello" and "My name is" the teachers all asked to take photos of us with the children and they were so friendly to us and literally did not want us to leave. The Japanese people that I met were kind and friendly, other than Manager.

It is impossible to put in words the beauty of the Japanese temples and the surroundings. There is the most incredible feeling of tranquility when you are in the vicinity and the temples are sublimely beautiful often surrounded by Zen gardens.

I went to several temples and experienced several different Japanese festivals or 'matsuri' as they are called in Japanese. Japanese festivals are usually connected to special historical events, fertility rites or prayers to the Gods for good health. At the start of the New Year, everyone visits the temple to pray for good fortune for the next 12 months. In mid January, there is a festival in Nagano, where offerings of snow are made to the Gods as a prayer for good crops for the year ahead, with dancing through the night.

One weekend not long before our contract ended, Jo and I were walking around the streets when we stumbled upon a wooden looking building with a sign saying in English 'CHURCH' we thought we must be dreaming! We decided to go inside and take a look, we always felt very safe in Japan anyway.

Imagine our shock when we found an English speaking husband and wife inside. We were so surprised and decided to go and join in the next church service. We only managed to go to a couple of services before we had to leave Japan but it was such a comfort finding something like that with other friendly English speakers and singing hymns. If only we had found It earlier.

Japan was truly a wonderful adventure for me, this beautiful country steeped in mythical traditions and modern wonders really is somewhere that must be visited to appreciate the true beauty and culture. While writing this book, The Hotel is still there and is now called Ito-en Hotels Riverside Uedakan. I would love to return as a guest one day with my family and visit Togura Kamiyamada again.

As we hugged and kissed our teacher friends Goodbye, there were lots of tears.

I left Togura Kamiyamada, with fists full of saved Yen and super skinny thanks to all the bike riding. It was dark and late when we arrived in the bustling city of Tokyo; we went out for some food and then went back to the Hotel, since we needed to get up super early for our flight home the following morning. We were all super excited to be going home to our families for a few weeks.

CHAPTER FIFTEEN

Jersey 3

S ummer season three started in Jersey.

We were rehearsed and ready to start our touring show The Cockney show. It was wonderful to be dancing with Rachel, and Anya again; there were just three dancers in the touring show, with myself as dance captain. Tony had been trained and was to be our sound technician accompanying the show on tour. Also in the show we had some very talented new acts, Paul Adams was a young up and coming Comedian, this was his first professional gig, having worked his way up through the ranks starting as a Bluecoat at Pontins. Paul was a really friendly guy, he recently came to perform in Dubai and we met up. Whilst reminiscing he told me that apparently I used to tell him off a lot in the show, I was his first ever dance captain. So sorry Paul!

There was also a husband and wife singing duo called Biloxy blues, Aisla was a talented and glamorous singer, her husband Steve accompanied her as the keyboard player. Steve and Aisla were a professional and polished duo. If ever we popped in to see them at home, Aisla would be running around cooking and waiting on Steve hand and foot. Steve would sit and start eating his food and say things like "Aisla, bit more butty on me tattey, love." I would describe him as the stereotypical 'Northern' man. She would lovingly get up and run to the kitchen to fetch the butter for him. People always think that show people must live incredibly glamorous lives, but the reality is often far from it. What you see on stage is not who we are off stage. On stage we are selling a dream, a beautiful fantasy.

Dick had two touring shows that year and in the other show was a dark haired girl called Lisa who I became close friends with and nicknamed 'Ladybird' We were all back living at 34 Seaton Place but in different rooms this year. I didn't stay living there for many weeks at all because a few weeks in to the summer season I met a local man called Robert. He was kind and genuine and after dating for a few weeks, he very quickly asked me to move in with him, which I did. It was strange not living at Seaton Place, it was strange not having to wait for the washing machine to be free or going to the fridge and find that someone had used up your milk or eaten your food.

Not long after I moved in with Rob, I was trying to cook something and I forgot that I had left some chips in the deep fat fryer whilst answering the phone and getting engrossed in a call.

After around 10 minutes the smoke alarm started going off and the whole kitchen ceiling was in flames. I called the fire station that thankfully were very nearby to where we lived in Queens Road, and came to put out the fire. The whole house stank of smoke and the cream carpets had to be professionally cleaned and the walls painted due to smoke damage. I felt terrible, I had only just moved in. Rob was calm and kind about it all thankfully.

That winter, I decided to stay in Jersey with Rob. Since I was in a committed relationship, I no longer wanted to go off dancing for a long winter season. Luckily, Caesars Palace was opening briefly for a Christmas show, and I was asked to be one of the dancers *and* the choreographer. I was so excited, my first job as a paid choreographer.

Rob and I flew off for a holiday to Jamaica for 2 weeks and in the afternoon, I would escape the Caribbean sun and go back to our suite and start choreographing the routines. I loved having the creative freedom to now be the choreographer myself. I spent hours and hours creating and perfecting routines and got so much satisfaction out of finding exactly the right moves to perfectly interpret the right section of music. I thought about our costumes or props that we would use and how best to use them while showcasing our talent as dancers. I had so much experience by now to draw upon from my years dancing.

In the Christmas show there were three dancers, me, "Ladybird" Lisa and another Lisa who Id become friends with, Paul Adams the Comedian and two well-known Singers, Diane Cousins and Martin Kelly.

We had lots of fun doing this show and it was wonderful to be performing on the Caesars Palace stage again, although this really would be the last time, since soon after it was sold to a property developer and the land was developed into residential homes.

Once the Christmas show finished, I worked at Chex again while trying to organize dancing work for the next summer season. As much as I loved dancing and working with my friends, Rachel, and Anya, I just did not enjoy doing the touring shows and decided to try and find dancing work in one of the other shows on the Island.

Luckily, Lisa told me that The Swanson's Hotel show on the Esplanade, where she was returning for the next summer season needed an additional dancer. I was offered the job and was very happy about this because it was a permanent show in a cabaret room, so no touring and the money was much better than all the other shows in Jersey I was surprised and pleased to discover.

Swanson's Hotel, Black and White Minstrel Show

Swanson's were doing a traditional black-and-white minstrel show. The entire cast was very talented with excellent singers, magic acts and a comedian.

Two mornings a week, we had to stand in St. Helier town center and give out leaflets promoting our show in our beautiful show costumes. We had a bright yellow piano that played songs from the show and we would push the yellow piano with the music blaring out up the main high Street to our pitch in the center of town. The tourists absolutely loved it and would ask for photos with the piano and us. Pam the wardrobe mistress would stand on guard and tell us off if we chatted to each other.

Apparently, the boss had bugged the dressing rooms a couple of years before I joined the show so that he could hear what people were saying about him! I don't believe there were any microphones in the dressing rooms the year that I was there, but we suspected that Pam was basically there instead of the microphones, a bit like a strict headmistress!

Year after year the shows were closing one by one, there were far less tourists coming to Jersey, because realistically for the same money you could fly to Spain and be guaranteed hot sunny weather for your holiday. It was quite expensive to get to Jersey by air or sea and the accommodation, food and drinks were not cheap either compared to European holiday destinations.

As each show closed down, I tried to find another to dance in.

I also decided that I needed to try to widen my options. Towards the end of the summer season, I decided to study for my R.S.A. Exercise to music fitness teacher diploma, together with my lovely cousin Juliette.

This was one of the best decisions that I have ever made.

I found it a bit of a struggle getting up early in time for the classes some days after the late night shows, but it was definitely worth it.

Juliette and I both passed with flying colours and this enabled us to teach any type of exercise to music.

I have used this qualification endlessly ever since I gained it all around the world.

At the very end of the season, I was approached by Diane Cousins to join her for the following summer season in an hotel called The Sunshine as a dancer and the choreographer.

Diane was going to be starring in the show along with a couple of other acts and there would be just two dancers, myself and a gorgeous dancer called Tara, who trained at Italia Conti.

The shows and budgets were sadly getting smaller and smaller.

Once spring rolled around, I flew over to the UK and hired the costumes through a contact of mine and excitedly started choreographing our routines.

The Sunshine Hotel Show

Diane was incredibly talented with an amazing voice, very similar to the sound and style of Shirley Bassey. Di was also a very funny Comedienne as well, which made her act so brilliant.

Tara and me decided that we would give up smoking during the summer season, so we went and bought nicotine patches. The only thing was, we had to keep them on all day except when sleeping. Our costumes were very small and skimpy, so it was hard to find somewhere that the nicotine patches would not be seen.

During the show after one of her songs Diane would chat to the audience in her strong Welsh accent and say "The dancers are lovely aren't they, and they are giving up smoking and need to keep their patches on, can you guess where they put their patches...?" The audience always used to have a good chuckle at that.

I can now reveal that we put them at the back of our bikini bottoms, so they were hidden just above our actual bottoms in the small triangle area of sparkly fabric. We did give up smoking for a few months but both started again, afraid that we would gain weight.

During the season, I was excited to be booked to do a photographic modeling job for Jersey Pearl. I loved their jewellery and still do. They selected their preferred photos to be used in their next campaign and suddenly my face was appearing on car park scratch cards, full pages in the newspaper and even on the *side* of buses for several years!

Life was good overall, when I was not dancing Rob and I travelled to far away places and lived in a beautiful home, but somehow, I felt unfulfilled and I felt *guilty* for feeling like this.

I decided to go and see a psychic and Tara and I both booked appointments to see a local clairvoyant called Diane Postlethwaite. This lady was so respected and sought after that to obtain an appointment, we had to write to her requesting one and since she only saw a limited amount of people each month there was no guarantee of getting one. When we received our confirmations, we were both overjoyed.

My personal feeling is that when we go to see these people, we are searching for something, seeking answers or direction in our life.

Diane Postlethwaite started talking and she seemed to know and be accurate about a lot of details about my life, even though I had not told her anything. She looked at my palm and asked me to draw a hand of tarot cards. She then talked at length about what she saw in the cards that I had drawn and the meaning.

Many of the things that she said and predicted to me weren't what I *wanted* to hear, so when I left I remember thinking that she was not really very good.

Tara and I swapped notes to see if she had said the same things to us both, but in fact our readings and forecasts were very different. I put my reading in a safe place and thought no more of it. I forgot about it.

Life however keeps leading us on journeys that we would not necessarily *choose*.

A few years later when I looked at the reading again I was absolutely ASTONISHED.

Diane Postlethwaite had told me that I would leave Jersey and go to work in the UK on a contract; this would be successful and lead to more contracts. She saw ships and dolphins and lifejackets. She told me that I would have a son. She told me about people and characters good and bad, unpleasant ones. She told me about animals and named them. She described my future home in great detail.

At that time, because I had no intentions whatsoever of leaving Jersey I thought it was really all a load of rubbish.

It turned out to be unbelievably ACCURATE.

Psychics defy reason and there is no tangible evidence, but because of my own personal experience with Diane, I believe that some people do have the gift and ability to be psychic.

As the summer season ended, I was looking through *The Stage* for any shorter winter jobs in the UK, since there was nothing in Jersey. I found one for a Christmas show for a company called Showstoppers Worldwide Entertainments which sounded right up my street with fabulous costumes and showgirl feathers.

I told my friends Lisa and the other Lisa 'Ladybird' about the show and we all applied and were offered the job together which was fantastic news.

Showstoppers Worldwide Entertainments

Paul Walsh was the boss and owner of Showstoppers Worldwide.

Paul was a fabulously talented performer himself, having studied at The Italia Conti School and performed professionally in National UK tours, such as *Joseph and the Amazing Technicolour Dream Coat* and *The Rocky Horror Show*.

He then went on to be a choreographer and was the original chore-ographer for the band Take That.

Paul was from Alderley Edge in Cheshire and this was where he lived and ran his company from.

We did our rehearsals there in the scout hut or the town hall on London Road.

Paul and I became life long friends, until sadly Paul Died in September 2019. I was so pleased that I had flown from Dubai to the UK in March 2019 for a reunion with him and some of my other closest friends and dancers who had all worked for him with Showstoppers Worldwide. Paul was so happy to be with '*his girls*' as he always called all of us.

The world lost a creative genius, but heaven will be a whole lot more sparkly, fun and fabulous with Paul up there high kicking his way around and dressing everyone in feather backpacks and sequins.

Paul's wonderfully talented Mum Margaret, along with a couple of her friends made all of our fabulous, lavish costumes. Sitting around a big table in the front room surrounded by sewing machines, fabric, rhinestones, glue guns and jewels. I used to love listening to them all chatting away and laughing in their broad Mancunian accents, it felt like I had stepped into a scene from *Coronation Street*. "Oooh bloody 'ell I've lost me needle!" and "Barbara, whose turn is it t' mek a brew?"

Or "Right time for a fag break…" These ladies were hilarious and extremely talented seamstresses.

All of Paul's costumes were F.A.B.U.L.O.U.S. He did not do minimal. He spared no expense on his costumes. Paul always wanted everything to be glittering and bigger and better, we were extremely lucky to wear his creations.

The two Lisa's and myself started rehearsals and met all the other dancers, amongst them Machala and Hayley who I became great friends with.

The Christmas show was wonderful; the venue was called Tall Trees, which was situated, near to a very pretty town called Yarm in North Yorkshire England. It was the run up to Christmas so there were loads of companies being brought in by the bus load, all celebrating their Christmas parties.

Once the show ended, I returned to Jersey and started thinking about the choreography and costumes for the next summer season at The Sunshine Hotel. This time, rather than renting costumes, I had decided to buy and have new costumes made, by two fabulously talented costume designer friends, Nigel, and Simon from Jersey. I loved selecting the perfect fabrics as well as thinking about the demands of the choreography and how the costumes would appear on stage in motion. Nigel and Simon were masters and thought about every little detail.

Then, Paul phoned and offered me another very short 3-week contract on a Norwegian ship joining Hayley and Ladybird I jumped at the chance to go.

Norway

This was basically a short booze cruise from Newcastle over to Norway. Everyone drank lots of booze on board, got to see some beautiful Norwegian Fjords and the town of Bergen and then drank all the way back to Newcastle before loading their cars up with duty free booze and cigarettes.

Norway was clean, expensive and it rained a lot. We loved getting off the ship and spending the day in Bergen, a city full of quaint colourful painted wooden houses, next to the water or clinging to the hillsides overlooking the fjords.

I had great fun with Ladybird and Hayley, we had lots of free time and I would sometimes teach exercise classes on board just for the three of us to pass the time. We couldn't believe how much alcohol the Norwegian crew consumed including the Captain!

Rob came out to meet me at the end of the contract and I returned to Jersey and continued choreographing the routines for the summer season, searching for bentwood chairs and various other props, but somehow, my heart was not in any of it.

A few weeks later, Paul from Showstoppers Worldwide phoned me in Jersey and asked me if I knew a dancer to go on a 6 month Mediterranean cruise, one of the girls had to drop out last minute and the rehearsals were starting in three days. Paul knew that I was well connected and knew lots of dancers all around the world. I told him that I would call a few friends and get back to him and he said "That's great thanks Gaynie," as he always called me.

I paused for a moment and then said, "Actually, I'll do it."

My heart was beating fast realizing what I had just said.

I knew that it was the right decision though and I needed to get away from Jersey.

Paul was really shocked obviously. "What about your show?" he asked. I told him that everything was done and I would sort a replacement out, which I did.

I left Jersey to go and start rehearsals back in Alderley edge again. It was very sad saying goodbye to Rob. We both still cared enormously for each other, but we both knew it was the right thing to do and parted amicably.

JERSEY CAESAR'S PALACE, BATTLE OF FLOWERS:
(L-R) RACHEL, TONY, GAYNOR, CLAUDIA, JO, & ANYA

JERSEY CAESAR'S PALACE WITH WORLD FAMOUS DANCER, WAYNE SLEEP

JERSEY, ST. OUENS MANOR PHOTO SHOOT

JERSEY OPERA HOUSE STAGE, BENTWOOD CHAIR ROUTINE

RACHEL & GAYNOR AT CAESAR'S PALACE

JERSEY, SWANSON'S *BLACK & WHITE MINSTREL SHOW*

JERSEY, BACKSTAGE SWANSON'S: (L-R) GAYNOR, LISA, & JULIE-ANNE

JERSEY, SWANSON'S COCKNEY SHOW WITH SOME OF THE TALENTED CAST

JERSEY, HOWARD DAVIS PARK PHOTO SHOOT, EN POINTE

SWITZERLAND RETONIOS CASINO BACKSTAGE:
(L-R) NIKKI 'PICKLE', EMMA, ADELE, & GAYNOR

SWITZERLAND, BACKSTAGE RETONIOS CASINO WITH CANADIAN MIKE

JAPAN WITH THE GEISHAS

JAPAN, BACKSTAGE WITH DRUMMING MUSICIANS

JAPAN, BACKSTAGE WITH MAMASEN & HER DAUGHTER

JAPAN, MEETING THE SCHOOL CHILDREN

JAPANESE HOME COOKING

JAPANESE TEMPLE, FEELING TALL

CHAPTER SIXTEEN
Cruise Ships

M/V The Azur, Cabin P14, Zattere 1473, 30123, Venice

For rehearsals, I based myself with Mum and Dad in Stoke-on-Trent and either caught the train or would drive up and down to Alderley Edge each day. It was lovely to be dancing with Hayley again and meet the other dancers, Machala, Shani, and the two Nicholas, 'big Nic' the tallest and 'little Nic'. This group of dancers became like sisters, the friendships we made were so strong due to the intensity of living on a ship and doing everything together and of course, fortunately genuinely liking each other. I think the worst place to have to endure, working with someone that you didn't like, or rivalry and backstabbing would be on a cruise ship, since there really is no escaping each other. Paul had already asked Hayley to be dance captain before I agreed to do the contract, so once he knew at last minute that I was going to be in the show too, he made us both joint dance captains with different responsibilities to resume, which worked well.

During rehearsals I would sometimes stay over with Paul and Margaret at their house in the spare room. In the evening, Paul, myself and some of the other dancers would always end up walking to a lovely old English pub nearby called The Drum and Monkey. There were often footballers in the pub, not that I recognized any of them, but Paul did and would say *"OOOOh look Gaynie, there's so-and-so, I wouldn't kick him out of bed for eating crackers."* Many of them had bought huge houses in Alderley Edge due to its close proximity to the Manchester United football club where they played.

Rehearsals for the cruise ships were the most intense and exhausting ever, since we had so many different shows to learn. Most of our cruises were for 7 days and the passengers want to see a different show each night, we usually had one night off per week. So that meant learning lots of shows and choreography.

Paul asked me if I would choreograph a couple of the showgirl feather routines, which I was very excited about. One routine was to the very famous and well-known theme tune *Formidable* from the Moulin Rouge show of the same name and the other was to *Dreamgirls* from the show of the same name.

I loved choreographing showgirl routines and that specific style of choreography, regal and elegant, is my favourite, which I had many years of experience by now from performing in the big European shows.

I created graceful dance routines which combined showing off our magnificent costumes and our dancing skills, for the audience to wonder at.

After around three weeks of rehearsals in Alderley Edge we were ready to leave and go and join the ship in Venice.

Very early in the morning we all met at Manchester airport, dressed in matching black 'Showstoppers Worldwide Entertainments on tour' sweatshirts. We must have looked quite striking, 6 tall dancers all dressed in black tour clothes and Paul the boss. We checked in our luggage along with lots and lots of trunks containing all of our show costumes.

For one routine we were wearing huge silver sparkling Statue of Liberty hats that had battery packs in and lit up. The trunk that they had been packed into we were told was just too big to go on the plane so we had to take them out of the trunk and carry one each as hand luggage. It's so funny to think of this now, it would be never be allowed these days especially with batteries in the hats. We boarded the plane trying not to poke anyone's eyes out with the pointy headdresses, panicking because we were running late and had a connecting flight. In Belgium we were frantically running through the airport to our next flight with the Statue of Liberty hats in our hands and Paul shouting at us, "Come on, girls, move your fannies!"

We arrived in Italy and were taken to the Cruise ship terminal. We stood on the quay in Venice in the blazing sun, sweating in our black sweatshirts, all looking up at the cruise ship *The Azur* which was to be our home for the next few months.

A company called Festival Cruises, who no longer exist, owned The Azur. They had several cruise ships in their fleet at the time. The Captain was Greek and most of the senior officers were too, with the rest of the crew and staff from practically every corner of the world.

As soon as we were allowed to get on the ship, we were taken directly to a staff area and had to lug our extremely heavy suitcases to our cabins, which were situated, on one of the lower decks. Only the Captain and high-ranking senior officers live on the higher decks of the ship.

There were two girls per cabin, Hayley and I had agreed to share a cabin, Shani was with little Nic and Machala and big Nic were sharing. The cabins were tiny with no windows. We had a bunk bed, a small single wardrobe each and one sink with a light over the mirror. There was a toilet and shower, which opened from both sides, which the girls behind us in another cabin also shared with us. It's amazing how quickly you can adapt to living in such a small space. Shani had recently been on another cruise contract and she had given us lots of great ideas to maximize the storage in the cabin. We used hanging shoe racks on the back of the door and crammed them full with toiletries and we had small kitchen storage trolleys that would usually hold vegetables, at the end of our bunk beds to put other things in like hair dryers and food snacks.

The cabins were so small that we had to take it in turns to dress or put our make up on, so if I was standing up putting my make up on or getting dressed, Hayley would sit on her top bunk and vice versa I would lie on my bottom bunk if she was moving around the cabin. Hayley and I really took pride in our cabin and when we had been paid we both went into Venice and bought lovely matching quilted blankets to put on our bunk beds, we made it look very cute.

The cabin walls were paper thin, so we could literally talk to Shani and little Nic who were the other side of us through the wall.

We immediately unpacked and organized all of our costumes in the dressing room behind the stage in the showroom and started rehearsing on the stage. The show room and stage were small compared to the ones that I have seen recently on cruise ships.

Our first shows were a huge success, everyone on board the ship was impressed with the caliber of choreography and costumes, and the show-room was packed. We performed two shows each night, one directly after each dinner sitting.

On our first night at sea, we went into the disco with Paul for cele-bratory drinks.

Paul had stayed on board with us for the first cruise to help us settle in and debuted our shows. He loved eyeing up the male crew members and passengers; he took great care with his appearance and reaped the benefits. He usually always had an adventure to tell us at breakfast from the night before!

There were several Greek officers at the bar, all looking extremely handsome, deeply suntanned in their white uniforms with stripes on the epaulettes depicting their seniority and rank.

They swarmed around us like bees around a honeypot, because we were the new girls on the ship and the dancers. I ended up chatting to a junior officer who came to sit beside me and introduced himself as Nikos. He was from Piraeus and it turned out that his father was a captain on one of the other Festival cruise ships. Nikos shared a cabin with another officer called Michalis who was chatting to big Nic. At the end of the night, we said goodnight and Nikos and Michalis invited myself and big Nic to meet them the following evening to go for drinks after we all finished work and we accepted.

Aside from doing our shows we had a few duties to do on the ship in the daytime, which the Cruise Director Franco allocated to us. My main one was taking fitness classes for people of all different ages, shapes sizes and nationalities. We also used to have to help with disembarkations at the various ports, which we thought was pointless since there were plenty of crew to actually oversee the safety of the passengers. Franco insisted though and wanted two of us to stand around smiling saying either *"have a nice day"* or *"welcome back on board"* Another pointless duty was sitting in the library, which we took in turns to do. I think I only ever saw 2 passengers come up in six months for a book. Everyone was far too busy enjoying themselves sunbathing, swimming, drinking, eating, doing quizzes or games while we were at sea, but library was a good chance to write letters back home to family and friends. One of our highlights was always receiving our post and letters from back home each time we docked back in Venice.

My favourite duty was the sail away party, which usually happened when we were departing Corfu. All of the dancers were required on the main deck to get the passengers up dancing, we would teach them to do popular line dances such as, the *Macarena* and *Saturday night* as we sailed away from Corfu, partying in the hot summer breeze.

Lifeboat Drills

There was quite a lot of safety training and drills. We did this each time new passengers embarked. Lifeboat drill always took a long time since the same announcement would need to be repeated in around 8 different languages.

I had to stand at the front of hundreds of passengers and demonstrate putting on the lifejacket correctly, the same as airline stewards do.

Then following that we would direct the passengers to the correct lifeboat station that they should go to in case of an emergency.

Luckily we never needed to put it into practice.

It was made very clear to us as soon as we started dancing on the ship that if we missed the ships departure then we were 100 percent responsible for the cost and organizing flying ourselves to the next port to catch up with the ship, so this was a good incentive to never be late. Cruise ships have to pay huge fines if they overstay their port time, so they won't wait. The only time that this almost happened for me was when I was walking around Venice one Saturday. I had allowed plenty of time to return to the ship, and after several months of walking around Venice, I thought I knew my way around easily. I got horridly lost. The small winding streets are like a maze. In another town you could flag down a taxi and get to the ship if this had happened, but that wasn't possible in Venice, you can only walk or get water taxis which did not go anywhere near the cruise ships. It was getting really late and I could feel my heart pounding in my chest as I tried unsuccessfully to find the right streets. My guardian angel was looking over me as usual and eventually with only a few minutes to spare I found the right route and ran back to the ship.

As dancers we were very lucky to have a lot of privileges that other crew and staff members did not. We were treated very well and could wear whatever clothes we wanted to and sit, eat and drink wherever we wanted to on the cruise ship, just like the passengers. Often the passengers would recognize us and they loved to chat to us and were interested to know about our life on board, we felt like mini celebrities on the ship. I loved the luxury of having all our food prepared and used it like a health retreat and ate small salads with a little blue cheese in most of the time. We of course had to keep ourselves thin. The passengers didn't need to worry about that though, they seemed to go from breakfast to lunch, afternoon tea, dinner, midnight buffet and any other snacks around the ship. They were on holiday though.

We did our weekly weigh ins down in the doctors medical centre and I had to fax our weights through to Paul each week. We all soon had a deep Mediterranean suntan, which also knocks half a stone off everyone's appearance.

Most of the crew ate in the crew 'mess' area. The officers were allowed to eat in the passenger areas too, but had to always be in full uniform.

The food was all-inclusive on the ship but alcohol was not. However, we had a 50% staff discount on everything on board and we were allowed to bring as much duty free as we wanted to on to the ship and consume it and so we did!

The First Date

The following evening after our two shows, big Nic and I trundled up to the library to meet Nikos and Michalis as arranged. "Ya sou" they greeted us in Greek They had brought wine with them and we moved outside to the top deck, it felt wildly romantic with the warm Mediterranean breeze blowing my hair around under the starry sky as the ship sailed. Nikos and I had an instant attraction and he was very different to anyone I had ever met with his interesting stories about growing up on cruise ships and his father being a Captain. Dating on board cruise ships is like dating in dog years, things progress about seven times faster. One month on a cruise ship feels like two years on the land. When you are living on a cruise ship you are working together, eating together and seeing each other every day whether you want to or not and it is difficult to find space to yourself, its very intense.

I had an inner sense that something important would come of this relationship which turned out to be right. Nikos ended up being the biological father of my amazing son Danny.

When people become couples on a cruise ship, other than the senior officers, no one has their own cabin, but the bunk beds have curtains that you pull across to make your bunk private. That does not make them sound proof though. Couples end up moving into each other's cabins and sharing small bunk beds together and alone time has to be scheduled between you and your roommate.

Nikos shared his cabin with Michalis, who turned out to be the sweetest person ever. Big Nic and Michalis did not become a couple after all, but remained friends.

Dimitris was their other good friend, he lived in the cabin opposite, we called him *Dimi*, an older guy who was also very kind and thoughtful and he had a huge crush on Machala. I adored all of the dancers on this contract, I definitely spent most of my time with Machala though and she became my closest friend.

She was always there for me to laugh with and cry on her shoulder when needed.

Often, myself, Nikos, Michalis, Machala and Dimi would get off the ship with some of the other dancers and go out together for Greek food and drinks. Even though we had good food free on board the ship, we still craved different food and these guys knew where all the best Greek taverns were.

We would feast on fresh fish or char grilled octopus washed down with ouzo. Ouzo is a strong aniseed flavoured liquor aperitif made in Greece. It is clear in the bottle but when you add a splash of water it turns cloudy. At first I hated the taste but after several tastings it started to grow on me. They ordered meatballs *'keftedes'* and Greek Salads, loaded with Feta cheese and olives, and *'Tyropitas'*, delicious cheese pies made with layers of buttered filo pastry.

We sipped on *'Frappe'*, refreshing iced Coffees, which seemed to be the National drink and part of the lifestyle and culture.

We also discovered *Baklava*, made from layers of filo pastry and filled with chopped nuts, cinnamon, sugar and butter and soaked in honey syrup. All of our Greek friends loved to claim that Greeks invented Baklava, but if you ask Turkish people or Arabic people they will say the same thing.

Each culture has its own variation of this delicious desert and I really don't care who invented it, I'm just glad that they did!

There were always cabin parties going on every night, when the staff on cruise ships are not working they drink and party most of the time.

We started to all congregate in either Nikos and Michalis cabin or Dimitris's cabin which was just across the corridor. All of the cabins are small, but it's amazing how many of us we could squeeze in sitting on the floor and on cushions and bunk beds. Somehow we even found space to dance if a good song came on.

The Greek men were all passionate about Greek dancing; they claim that they can dance by the time they can walk. This style of *Zeibekiko* dancing is done individually to traditional Greek songs, not in circles to upbeat music as you might see at a restaurant for tourists. At first I thought it was the most bizarre thing Id ever seen. There is no set choreography, no set steps, no particular rhythm; it is an improvised dance that expresses the feelings of the individual who gets up to dance. The songs that they would dance too were obviously all sang in Greek, but they would explain to us some of the lyrics, which are mainly about feelings of sadness, life's despair and unfulfilled dreams, maybe the bad luck that you foresee coming. Even without being able to understand the words, the music alone and the tone of the song and dancing lets you know that it is all very deep and emotional.

The man dances alone and it is a personal moment, it is an insult to interrupt the dance. While he dances, the other friends and we ladies would all clap slowly along with the song, with loud cries of *Oppa! Oppa!* Which is a great Greek utterance to express emotion.

Michalis had brought his traditional Greek musical instrument on board with him, the 'bouzouki' and was very talented at playing it. It had a highly distinctive sound and was beautifully and ornately decorated. It looked a bit like a Mandolin with a round wooden body and a long neck with strings on.

The cabin parties were brilliant fun and the alcohol flowed freely day and night in our cabins, we definitely had a much higher alcohol tolerance.

Living the Dream

There is something truly magical about waking up in a different port each day. I still feel like that now when I'm on a cruise. Running up the stairs to look over the railings of the ship, or opening the curtains and looking out of the window not knowing what you will see, is like opening up a surprise gift each day.

For the first few weeks, I felt as though I was living the dream, being paid to do what I loved most, whilst seeing the world with an incredible group of girls and meeting a handsome Greek sailor. We were paid well and since we had no outgoings, it was easy to save money if we chose to.

It was so interesting; I loved getting off the ship discovering new ports and places. We were always crossing through different time zones and adjusting our watches forward or back.

If Nikos was off duty we would often go out together to historical sites, shops and restaurants, he knew most of the ports and was a good tour guide, educating me in the history of the Islands and teaching me Greek words.

It is impossible to name a favourite port, since we went to so many and they were all so interesting in their own unique ways, offering different experiences.

The Greek Islands were the biggest surprise for me since I had never been to Greece before the cruise.

There are more than 5,000 Greek islands and islets. Each island has its own particular charm, offering beautiful whitewashed houses, Turquoise seas and the most romantic sunsets.

Santorini was definitely one of the most unique and beautiful islands, shaped by a volcanic eruption a few thousand years ago and famous for its blue domed churches and white washed houses perched on the edges of cliff top villages. You will most likely have seen pictures somewhere on Instagram or the Internet of Santorini, but they really don't do it justice I can assure you.

The Azur would anchor near to the old port in Fira and then we took a tender boat to get to the small port. After that we could either take a cable car or walk up around 600 steps to the town of Fira. The other option was to take a donkey, which we did. This was a lot of fun, but I did feel bad for the donkeys when I saw the size of some of the passengers they had to carry!

In Corfu, our Greek shipmates rented a car and drove us to Kanoni, just a few minute drive outside of Corfu town and we sat high on a hill and sipped cocktails while overlooking the small church of Panagia Vlacherna and Mouse Island, the most famous and photographed spot in Corfu.

The Greeks were hugely patriotic and extremely proud of their beautiful Islands and quite rightly so.

Piraeus port always had a special buzz of excitement about it, since it was the main port in Athens. The passengers would go and see the Acropolis and other sights of interest, while lots of the Greek crew went home for the day if they lived close enough, or their families came to visit them at the port. There was always delicious home made Greek food to eat on board after Piraeus that Grandmothers, mothers, wives and daughters lovingly brought for their seafaring men to enjoy a little taste of home at sea.

Week by week and month by month we would sail away from Venice and discover Naxos and Paxos, Crete, Kos, Piraeus, Santorini, Crete, Sicily, Corsica, Rome, Croatia, Malta, Naples, Livorno, Civitavecchia, Gibraltar, Malaga, Ibiza, Morocco, Tunisia, Alexandria, Marmaris and Bodrum, Cyprus, Casablanca, Lanzarote and many, many other ports, too numerous to recall on these wonderful adventures. I couldn't believe this was my job. I loved it.

For some of the other staff though, it was definitely not like our experience. We became good friends with the Indonesian laundry workers who lived deep down in the bowels of the ship. They toiled below the decks in the laundry, which never closed, and they hardly ever saw daylight. They were rarely allowed off the ship. There were Filipinos and Bangladeshi staff who chopped vegetables all day long and made bread and croissants and they were paid extremely low salaries and sleeping 6 people to each tiny cabin. Sometimes after our cabin parties at around 3 a.m. we would go on

impromptu trips to the bakery and beg for freshly made bread and croissants to smear Marmite on, since they baked all night long.

We had two cocktail nights each cruise, one at the beginning and one
at the end.

Last year when we went on Crystal Cruises for a holiday, I felt disappointed that many of the passengers did not bother to dress up for the
formal night any longer. In the same way, when I went to watch the Moulin
Rouge show recently, I also felt saddened to see tourists arriving to see the
show dressed casually in trainers with backpacks on. Many people seem to
have lost the desire to dress up and as a result these events no longer have
the same wonderful sense of occasion as they did previously.

The Captain always attended in his pristine uniform and the passengers loved meeting him and having the opportunity to have a photo taken
with him. The question that everyone always asked while the captain was
doing this was, "Who is sailing the ship?"

Whilst the Captain directs the piloting of the ship, the bridge sailors
are on shifts at the helm most of the time. The Captain has many duties, he
supervises the maintenance of the ship and upkeep and ensures that all the
maritime protocols and safety regulations are strictly followed and has the
final authority for everyone on board.

For the formal cocktail evenings, everyone was required to dress in
black tie and look very glamorous.

I loved it. The officers all loved it too, strutting around looking handsome in their white uniforms and eyeing up the passengers.

Relationships and Affairs on Board

It was common for many married crew members to have affairs with
people on the ship in addition to their partner at home. I always felt sad for
the wives who were being cheated on and humiliated by their husbands.
Often we would see wives and children come on board for a week or two
and everyone would play happy families and then as soon as the families
left, they would be straight back with their ship partner. Some couples had

'agreements' we learned, that they were allowed to have affairs with passengers, who would only be on the ship for a week or two at most usually, but were not allowed to have affairs with other crew members, in case they fell in love. Nowadays, due to rape claims it is strictly forbidden for crew to have a relationship with a passenger. Some crew members even tried to have two onboard partners simultaneously. Nikos, I soon found out, unfortunately fell into that category.

After a few happy weeks together, head over heels or so I thought, he started to act strangely and would say he had to work extra hours or do more training or cover someone's shift. I soon found out that he was secretly sneaking off to the cabin of a single Swiss female passenger. I was hurt and humiliated and we split up instantly. It was really hard because it was difficult not to see or bump into each other around the ship. What made it worse was that he didn't even try to be discreet about it and as soon as we would disembark in ports, I would see them leaving the ship hand in hand, wrapped around each other and kissing for the whole world to see.

After the Swiss passenger disembarked, within a few days he was begging to get back together with me, declaring it was all a big mistake and he realised how foolish he had been.

I chose to believe and forgive him and give him another chance, he had quite an addictive and charismatic personality and the pursuit of love can be blinding.

For a while things went back to normal and I was blissfully happy, but there were plenty more ups and downs to come. Nikos suddenly announced that his former girlfriend, a Dutch dancer, was coming on board for a cruise and they had 'unfinished business that they needed to resolve'. I was absolutely stunned. I watched again as without the blink of an eye he switched seamlessly from me to her and they paraded around the ship arm in arm.

I would never have given him more chances if I had not been stuck on a cruise ship, in the real world I would have been able to move on, but on a ship its hard when you live 10 feet away from each other.

Another time, I heard that he was playing around with a pretty Swedish passenger while we were doing our shows. I asked my friend on reception to find out her cabin number, which she did, obviously this was not really allowed but we all looked out for each other on board, like a sisterhood. Well, most of us anyway.

I caught him red handed once more. He always had girls swooning over him, there was just something about him that was irresistible and he knew it.

He was very good at sweet-talking me into giving him yet another chance, he would declare his complete stupidity, apologize and say that he had learned and that he would change and that he only wanted to be with me, *forever.*

Most of the sailing was blissful but occasionally we had rough seas. I felt very seasick when the ship was rocking and rolling, but *the show must go on as* the saying goes and it did. We would tone down the choreography a little and cut out a few cartwheels and things to minimize injuries. It was still hard though stumbling and trying to balance whilst doing a cancan routine or an elegant showgirl feather routine.

One of my favourite routines was a solo that I performed to a song called *Man wanted* from the musical Copacabana. In a red polka dot bikini and a large over the top blonde curly wig, I would high kick and 'chaine' turn after turn around the stage at a fast pace, whilst playback (miming) singing to the track *"Man wanted one, real man wanted, one mister rough and tough … oh kiss me till I cry Ooh!"*

During this routine I had to pretend to get disorientated and land up sitting on the lap of a male passenger sat on the front row, on rough sea days there was no pretending, I would often sway and fall into a lap and feel relieved to sit down for a few seconds, while the wife and family would frantically try to take photos.

For my birthday, the girls all decorated my cabin door with balloons and messages, it was such a lovely surprise to wake up to and so thoughtful of them. We were in the port of Kos on my birthday and Nikos and I, along with Michalis, Dimi, Machala all went for drinks and then I celebrated again with all of the dancers and a few others on the ship after our shows.

Dimi and Michalis bought me the most beautiful gold chain and Crucifix for my birthday, it was hand made in a jewelry workshop that adjoined a church in the Island of Rhodes where we sometimes docked. Not only was it very striking to look at and admire, I always felt that the cross had special powers and it became known around the ship, a few people asked to touch my cross for luck when needed, maybe if a member of their family was ill or they needed something.

Towards the end of the cruise, the captains changed over and Nikos's father came and took over as our Captain on The Azur. Captain V. was an all-round unpleasant character. He strutted around the ship like a rooster in a hen house and cheated on his wife regularly and openly in front of his son. No wonder really that Nikos thought that was 'normal' and behaved in the same way then, he had not had a good role model at all.

We were sailing around the Eastern Mediterranean now and about to dock in Egypt, I had always wanted to see the pyramids. Unfortunately Captain V. would not allow any of us to disembark because he considered it was too risky due to tourists being targeted by terrorists recently, we were saddened by this news but understood the logic.

The contract was coming to an end. One of our last ports was Haifa in Israel. Machala and I decided that we would go on the organized excursion and bought our tickets.

There was something magical, discovering the land that we had grown up learning and singing hymns about. We took a coach from Haifa port to the Mount of Olives, where some of the olive trees are over 900 years old. Next, we walked around the city of Jerusalem hearing the history and discovering the four quarters ending up at the Western wall, sometimes called the wailing wall. The tradition here is to place slips of paper containing written prayers to God into the cracks of the old wall. Machala and I took some paper, wrote our prayers and placed them into the wall and sat and paused briefly on one of the chairs nearby for a moment of prayer and reflection.

Next, we continued on to Bethlehem and the church of the Nativity where Jesus was born. We stopped briefly at a shop and I bought some carved olive wood Christmas tree decorations, which I have used ever since on my Christmas tree. It was mid November now, and I remember thinking that in two or three weeks, adults and children all around the world, would soon be singing the famous hymns about the nativity and this very place, "O little town of Bethlehem," "Silent night," "Away in a manger," and "We three kings".

It really felt very special to be here.

The end of the cruise was approaching, *The Azur* was due to go into dry dock for some routine maintenance and Paul offered us to return to *The Azur* for the next contract which would start after around a 3 week rehearsal period in Alderley Edge. Alternatively, we could take other dancing contracts around the world with Paul or other companies. None of the other dancers decided to return, they all chose to go and explore different countries.

I decided that I was not ready to give up on Nikos yet and would return for the next contract.

The 'Dreamgirls' all flew back together and hugged each other farewell as we went our separate ways on to numerous new adventures.

Cruise II

There was another hectic rehearsal period, learning the new choreography and shows. Paul had choreographed several solo routines for me to perform or made me the principal dancer in several of the routines; this gave me a few minutes to really showcase my own individual style, which I enjoyed the extra buzz from.

I quickly organized Christmas gifts to leave for my family and then said farewell and flew back out to join the ship with the new group of dancers.

This time we joined the ship in Genoa, I was counting the hours down until I would be together with Nikos, we had spent the time apart phoning each other whenever we had chance.

As soon as I was back on board, he was fussing over me with adoration and affection, and for a while we were very happy together and loved up again.

Our itineraries were more to the South and East Mediterranean, or around the Canary Islands, chasing the warmer weather. Christmas was approaching very quickly; Nikos and I decorated the cabin with a tiny Christmas tree and we all placed gifts around it.

On New Years Eve after our shows had finished and approaching midnight, we all went out on deck in the beautiful port of Funchal in Madeira. We celebrated the start of the New Year with lots of other cruise ships all anchored in the Atlantic Ocean, drinking champagne and looking up at the sky at the memorable fireworks.

I settled back into ship life, it was much the same but with new shows and new people. It was lovely to see Michalis and Dimi again and a few other familiar friends from the previous cruise contract.

The new dancers were a great bunch of girls and excellent dancers.

I spent most of my time with Nikos though and he did not want me to enjoy myself with the other dancers. He had become very dominant and manipulative.

Our relationship was basically the same cycle of ups and downs, highs and lows.

At the end of our contract, Nikos was going to do his military service, which was still compulsory in Greece. He had delayed this for several years but now needed to do it. He asked me to go with him and I agreed. I was excited to do something different.

After 12 years of non-stop dancing and travelling since I left school, I wanted to settle down and craved a taste of 'normality'.

Cruising had been a wonderful dancing adventure for me. Depending on your personality, it can be a dream job. Some of my friends have worked on there for more than 20 years now; it is very easy to get stuck in the easy lifestyle and the money that you can save. Everything is done for you, no cooking, cleaning or laundry, after so many years on board they say that it becomes hard to adjust to living on the land.

Whilst Nikos was doing his initial training for the military, I busied myself back In the UK. Choreographing for Paul, doing odd modeling jobs and promotion work and learning Greek. I was excited to be booked for a modeling job at Manchester United football club with a girl called Emma, they were launching their own brand of champagne and we appeared in all of the daily newspapers the following day pictured with Martin Edwards, the chairman at the time on the pitch and some of the players. We stayed for lunch, I remember Gary Rhodes, the well-known chef had paired the Champagne with the menu, he was sat on our table and was delightful to chat to.

TALL TREES SHOW FOR SHOWSTOPPERS WORLDWIDE, PINK & BLACK FEATHERS

TALL TREES, *RELIGHT MY FIRE* ROUTINE

AZUR CRUISE SHIP FOR SHOWSTOPPERS WORLDWIDE, QUEEN OF THE SEA

AZUR CRUISE SHIP, RED & YELLOW WHEEL FEATHERS

AZUR CRUISE SHIP, BRONZE & BLACK FEATHERS

ATHENS, MEETING THE LOCALS!

ME AND MY 'DREAMGIRLS':
(L-R) 'BIG' NIC, SHANI, GAYNIE, HAYLEY, MACHALA, & 'LITTLE' NIC

Chios Island

Nikos found out that he was going to be stationed in the Island of Chios. We could not have been happier about this, since this was the Island that our dear friend Michalis was from. I made my way back to Greece and caught the ferry from Piraeus to Chios.

Chios is one of the most interesting places that I have ever discovered. I loved this Island.

The kidney shaped island is the 5th largest Greek Island and is situated in the northern Aegean sea, and only 12 km away from the Turkish port of Cesme.

The most unique thing about Chios is the *'mastica'* produced there, which is the sap of the mastic trees. Its nickname is "The Mastic Island" the mastic resin is used to flavor food and drinks and used to help digestion and you can get all sorts of mastic products, everything from gum, toothpaste, sweets and many varieties of ouzo. No other region has ever been able to reproduce the taste of Chios mastic due to the microclimate in Chios. It really is a treasure.

When I first descended the ferry in Chios, I thought, *wow, where am I? What kind of place is this?* It was so old fashioned, with a derelict old theatre that you could still just about read the faded painted name of "Rex theatre." Old style ouzerie bars dotted along the waterfront, filled with old men playing backgammon and cards. In the evenings there were always a large number of young soldiers, who were allowed out of the camps for a few hours, doing their obligatory military service, as was Nikos.

I quickly realised that Chios town is actually somewhere that you should ideally just pass through on your way to discover the real beauty of Chios.

We found a small studio to rent in the town and then when Nikos was in the camp, I walked around the small town and knocked on the doors of gyms and somehow managed to find myself work teaching fitness classes. I learned all the words in Greek that I needed to teach fitness, counting to eight, left and right, turn, again, well done. Nikos was obliged to live at the military camp with all of the other soldiers, but his senior officer heard that

I had come to the Island, which was unheard of, even for Greeks girls, let alone an English girl. He kindly allowed Nikos to stay out with me at the studio a couple of nights each week.

Even though it was a beautiful Island, if you have no one to talk to it is lonely. I busied myself as best as I could, teaching at the gym, cleaning the studio, hand washing my clothes and his uniform, since we had no washing machine, and learning to cook Greek food, whilst counting down the hours until Nikos was free in the evening. I would buy phone cards and speak to Mum and write letters to friends.

Fortunately, our good friend Michalis was due to be back home in Chios soon to spend some time with his family.

It was wonderful having Michalis there, he treated me like his little sister and called me the same. He showed me around the Island on the back of his powerful motorbike, that I was a little bit terrified on, taking me to wonderful beaches and villages.

Michalis and his whole family made me feel so welcome, inviting me to their homes for food.

Cooking traditional delicious Chios foods, such as braised rabbit, baked Mastello cheese, local sausages and tomato keftedes.

I completely fell in love with the villages of Pyrgi and Mesta and loved hearing the history of these medieval villages from Michalis.

In the 'painted village' of Pyrgi, the façade of each building is ornately painted in black and white geometrical patterns known as *ksista*. Michalis told me that if you lived elsewhere in Greece and see a house decorated in *ksista* style then you know that the inhabitants are from Pyrgi. I loved seeing the local ladies sitting outside on their doorsteps, usually dressed all in black which I used to think must be very hot in the heat here, clean-ing the mastic in huge circular looking sieves. Most of the homes in Pyrgi had tomatoes hanging from beneath the balconies, drying in the hot sun. The streets were narrow and cobbled with archways. Pyrgi is believed to be the ancestral home of Christopher Columbus, he wrote about the Island of Chios and the healing properties of the mastic and there are many families in Pyrgi whose last name is Columbus. There are several churches and small chapels in Pyrgi village amongst them the 13th century Byzantine church of St. Apostles, I loved going inside the churches and chapels to light a candle and escape from the hot sun outside.

Mesta is a unique medieval fortress village in Southern Chios, This perfectly preserved village is nestled in a valley, deliberately out of sight from the sea and surrounded by high walls for protection from pirates and attackers. The pretty cobbled streets are far too narrow for vehicles; the sole means of transport is donkeys in the winding streets. Inside the walls, all of the houses are connected throughout the whole village and if you were to go on to the roof you can walk around the whole village from one roof to the next. Michalis told me that he used to do this as a young boy.

Around 300 people live here and several of Michalis family still lived there and invited us to have lunch with them, including his grandparents. What amazed me was that lots of the people in this village were all in their late 90's.

There must definitely be something about the healthy Mediterranean diet and this type of simplistic lifestyle that is very life prolonging. It certainly seemed as though these people had found the right recipe for a long life.

I was so lucky to have my dear friend here to show me around his beautiful Island.

Michalis and his family made my experience of Chios a memorable, lifetime experience.

Being stuck inside a military camp did not present Nikos with too many opportunities to philander. However, one night when he was allowed our for an overnight, we were out in a club drinking with Michalis and after a few drinks, he started shouting at me to go home in a taxi saying he wanted to have a 'boys night out'.

I couldn't believe it; I'd moved my whole life to be with him and support him on this remote Island where I spent most of my time *alone*.

I could tell that Michalis thought that he was out of order and was horrified.

I'm sure they never would have been friends if it weren't for the fact that they ended up sharing a cabin. They had such different values and behaviour.

As usual I forgave Nikos as he apologized the next day and filled me with promises of marriage after the army was finished.

This year, I spent my birthday entirely alone, Michalis had to leave and go back to join the cruise ship and Nikos was not allowed out from the army camp on that day. I thought back to how different it was to the previous year when the dancers had decorated my cabin door.

The weeks rolled by, mostly uneventfully, until November when I discovered that I was pregnant!

This was unplanned but we were both unbelievably happy and excited. On Christmas Eve in Greece, Nikos officially proposed to me with a ring and we hurriedly planned our wedding for the following April.

Nikos was allowed to defer the army and we moved to Stoke-on-Trent, to prepare for our big traditional white wedding and the birth of our child. I excitedly invited friends from all over the world who booked Hotels and flights ready to come and celebrate with us.

Nikos hated the UK and it was hard for him to adjust, which I could understand.

What I didn't understand was why as a father-to-be and now engaged to be married, he thought it was Ok to go out and get drunk and be unfaithful with other girls.

My younger brother and his friends even caught him red handed.

I was no longer blinded by love; the harsh truth had finally hit me. He would never change.

I called my wedding off 5 days before.

Five days before my planned wedding and six months pregnant, I somehow found the strength to cancel our wedding.

I will never be able to explain in words what that was like and how heartbroken I was at that time in my life, so I wont even try.

I kept myself busy, driving up and down the M25 to Alderley Edge doing lots of choreographing for Paul and helping him at auditions. He had so many contracts now all over the world that we were always auditioning. I thought back to all of the auditions that I had attended, I knew how these girls were feeling. There really is no such thing as a typical audition and no two auditions are ever the same obviously. A good or bad audition has the potential to change your life, in *so* many ways.

One day during rehearsals that I was choreographing for a cruise, Paul came in to watch and pulled me to one side to speak to me. He had noticed that one of the dancers was really struggling. She had a great physique and was extremely pretty, but simply wasn't a strong enough dancer and could not pick up the choreography and routines quickly enough. As mentioned before, there are so many routines and shows to learn for a cruise contract that you need to be able to do this quickly. I had noticed too, but was hoping that she would somehow relax and speed up. Paul told me that he wanted me to release her. I had the horrid task of telling her that evening that she had to leave. I did my best to explain to her that she would be great for another contract where there was only one show to learn. She was understandably upset though and crying and shouting at me rudely. I understood, she was hurting and needed someone to blame.

I continued choreographing and doing the French cancan throughout my entire pregnancy, so no wonder Dan loves music and dancing.

My amazing son was born on August 5th 1998.

Unengaged and unmarried, Nikos and I stayed together after the birth of our son for a while.

Relationships with children are worth the fight, so I did this.

Fighting to hold on to someone who is not fighting to hold on to you is impossible though. Nikos simply went back to his life in Greece and on cruise ships as if we had never existed.

I will never regret my relationship with him and hope that he found happiness.

We were both young and I think Nikos was a good person at heart, he just had poor examples to learn from.

CHAPTER SEVENTEEN

New Beginnings

New beginnings are often disguised as painful endings

My son Danny has been a blessing from the moment he was born and still is. He is a ray of sunshine and has filled my life with unbelievable love, joy and happiness.

As a single mother, I continued my life with my delightful son, working as a choreographer for Paul whenever possible.

Financially and emotionally it was really difficult for me for many years alone.

Mum and Dad decided to move to Weymouth and bought a small guesthouse, so Dan and I went with them. It was time for me to "re-invent" myself, I attended college at night learning computer skills and worked at a local newspaper in the daytime and taught dance classes to children and ladies.

Weymouth was a lovely, carefree seaside town to live in for a few years with a toddler.

Mum and Dad then decided to move back to Jersey to retire and Dan and I decided to go too.

Somewhere in the middle of my ordinary life in Jersey, a fairytale happened and I met my husband Tom.

The most wonderful man that I have ever met.

You did not play silly games and showed me your true love and commitment by your *behaviour*.

You *chose* to be a father to Dan. A GREAT Dad.

Tom and I decided to get married in a very small intimate ceremony at the Wynn Hotel in Las Vegas with Dan as Best Man.

My heart was bursting with happiness, committing it to memory, breathing it all in.

Our beautiful daughter Genie was born two years later, and our family was complete.

"You can take the girl out of the show, but you can't take the show out of the girl."

I still love to go and watch shows.

Over the last 20 years, showgirl numbers have declined drastically because so many of these glamorous shows have now been lost and closed forever.

There are various reasons for this, changing tastes and the high costs of the shows.

Dancers train for years to have the opportunity to perform and entertain spectators and I feel *incredibly* lucky to have had this wonderful dancing career.

I hope that you enjoyed reading about it.

Acknowledgements

Thank you to my wonderful Mum, Wendy for always encouraging me, helping me, believing in me, and sitting for hours on end through auditions and rehearsals. To Dad in heaven for working so very hard, enabling me to go to dancing school. To my dear brothers Adey and Chalky for coming to see my shows and being great Brothers and Uncles.

To my friends mentioned in the book, and in my current life, thank you for your valued friendship.

Thank you to my wonderful son Dan, who made me believe that people might want to hear these stories and who encouraged me to keep writing, as we shared an office during the COVID lockdown 2020.

Thank you to my adorable daughter Genie, who continuously asks and loves to hear the same stories, over and over about Mummy dancing on a big stage and wearing pretty costumes, usually when we are in the car together.

Thank you to my wonderful husband, Tom, for helping me in so many ways with my first publishing experience. I am proud to be your wife every day. Thank you for loving me for who I am. I often wish that I had met you sooner in my life, to be able to love you for longer.

If I had, then the stories in this book would not exist.